A New York Times Book Review Editors' Choice
An Indie Next pick
A Chicago Tribune Editor's Choice
A USA Today New and Noteworthy selection
One of Barnes & Noble's Unforgettable Memoirs of 2013
A Kirkus Best Books of the Year selection for Nonfiction

Praise for
MY MISTAKE

"Menaker's dishy, behind-the-pages look at The New Yorker magazine would be enough to highly recommend his new book, but, for this reader, his ruminations on memory (at the heart of this and any memoir) are even more striking." — Seattle Times

"Funny and lighthearted ... Menaker gives readers a glimpse into the less-than-rarefied world of fiction — publishing, marketing, buying and selling. And it's fascinating." — Washington Post

"Set in the world of literary New York, [My Mistake] is undeniably insider-y and gossipy ... But the human experiences he describes — especially the hard stuff, like family, illness and death — will be familiar to anyone." — NPR.org

"A wild ride that will provide insider glimpses of the New York publishing world from 1969 onward, with the author serving as one of the scene's principal participants and sharpest observers ... Not easy to pigeonhole, this is an amalgam of autobiography and cultural history at its best." — BookPage

"In this insightful memoir, Menaker leads his readers down the hallowed halls of *The New Yorker* . . . But the book isn't all business. Menaker also delves into the ups and downs of his personal life, from summers at his uncle's camp, to the death of his mother."

—*Real Simple*

"[A] beguiling sketch of a literary life . . . [and] a wryly personal history of magazine and book publishing over the past four decades. A–"—*Entertainment Weekly*

"In this dynamic memoir, Menaker, the former editor of *The New Yorker*, offers a moving rumination . . . [and] deconstructs a hardworking life, which has had its share of luck, triumphs, and tragedies, in prose that is impassioned, witty, and lovely. Do not miss this one."—*The Barnes & Noble Book Blog*

"[Menaker] is an expert at turning those proverbial life-lemons into lemonades; his description of his protracted recent struggle with lung cancer, for example, winds up being one of the memoir's most inspiring and invigorating sections."—*Paris Review*

"A well-known editor's funny and thoughtful memoir of wrong turns, both in and out of publishing . . . Menaker doesn't just recount experiences; he digs away at them with wit and astute reflection, looking for the pattern of a life that defies easy profit-and-loss lessons."—*Kirkus Reviews*, **starred review**

"Menaker's memoir captures a pair of lost worlds: the old lefty Greenwich Village, where he grew up in the 1940s and 1950s, and the byzantine kingdom of *The New Yorker*, where he worked for twenty-six years, mostly during the peculiar editorship of William Shawn."—*Johns Hopkins Magazine*

"Menaker is at his best when irreverent: chuckling at aptronyms (people aptly named), or deflating *New Yorker* legends (William Shawn and Tina Brown, most notably). Still, in this book of years, gossip is secondary to the writer's own musings and memories. Menaker leaves the reader with a sense of the vast triumph that is a life well lived." — *Publishers Weekly*

"He tells that story in *My Mistake*, with a breezy wit and fascinating insider portraits of people with whom he has worked over the years . . . A charming and revealing insider's look at the world of *The New Yorker* and big-time book publishing." — *Shelf Awareness*

"[A] sparkling gem of a memoir . . . The writing simply shines; it's at once jaunty and erudite. I kept wondering, 'How does he do that?' " — *San Francisco Chronicle*

"The story of how one intelligent and sensitive man has carried on with patient good humor in the face of an ample share of what life hands out in the way of both sadness and joy . . . [A] lively and life-affirming book." — *Bookreporter*

"More than just gossip from [the] publishing world . . . Menaker has a lot of stories to tell." — *Boston Globe*

"[Menaker]'s bold enough to explore his years at *The New Yorker*, where he stayed for twenty-six years despite discouragement from William Shawn, and the perpetual self-doubt that has dogged him, particularly owing to his role in his brother's inadvertent death. Certainly of interest to memoir fans and literati." — *Library Journal*

"[Menaker] contemplates the origins, happenstance, and consequences of his devotion to literature in a warm, humorous, on-point memoir. Amiably self-deprecating, Menaker is a deft sketch artist, vividly portraying loved ones (especially his older brother, who goaded him to excel and whose early death is the source of depthless sorrow) and colleagues (his portraits of *New Yorker* staff are hilarious, barbed, and tender). His insider view of publishing is eye-opening and entertaining." —*Booklist*

"Mov[es] along briskly ... There are enough industry anecdotes to keep any book-person eagerly reading, but the deeper current—of a man genuinely assessing his life—will stay in the memory longer." —*Open Letters Monthly*

"*My Mistake* will have particular appeal for those interested in literary culture (and, in particular, *The New Yorker*'s role in shaping it), but one hopes it garners a wider audience, because Menaker is excellent company and he tells his story well."

—*Gazette* (Eastern Iowa)

"Full of fantastic anecdotes about the people behind so many notable bylines over so many years ... [and] Menaker draws us in just as closely with the more personal material on his family."

—*Connecticut Post*

"*My Mistake* is only sometimes rueful. It is also frequently funny and splendidly precise as it takes a look back at a life led in the world of magazine editing and book publishing, a behind-the-scenes rumination of a time gone by. Intriguing now, it will be necessary later; readers will be thankful for this quirky and delightful piece of history." —**Elizabeth Strout, Pulitzer Prize winner and best-selling author of *Olive Kitteridge* and *The Burgess Boys***

"Daniel Menaker's distinctive journey through his own memories is impossible to resist—and not just for those of us with an appetite for literary anecdote. *My Mistake* is also the story of literary New York, with keen, vivid impressions from Menaker's forties childhood, Cold War coming-of-age, and long career at the epicenter of the publishing industry during the onslaught of the Digital Age."

—Jennifer Egan, best-selling author of *A Visit from the Goon Squad*

"I can't remember when I've read a memoir this—let's say 'soulful.' Funny, sad, and wryly self-aware, Menaker shines a bright light on his own background, our literary life, and his own path through it."—James Gleick, best-selling author of *The Information*

"*My Mistake* brings to mind the poetic prose of James Agee. Menaker's stories of life as fiction editor at *The New Yorker* and Random House are a delight, the way he tells them simply perfect. Humorous, thoughtful, heartbreaking, and brave. I have not enjoyed a memoir more."—Julie Klam, *New York Times* best-selling author of *Please Excuse My Daughter*

"How can something written so accurately be so witty? Don't you have to cheat a bit to wring the humor out of life? Daniel Menaker has constructed a compelling tale that irises down to a powerful and emotional climax and is delivered in exacting prose woven into affecting poetry."—Steve Martin

MY MISTAKE

My Mistake

A MEMOIR

Daniel Menaker

Mariner Books
Houghton Mifflin Harcourt
BOSTON   NEW YORK

First Mariner Books edition 2014

Copyright © 2013 by Daniel Menaker

www.hmhco.com

Library of Congress Cataloging-in-Publication Data
Menaker, Daniel.
My mistake / Daniel Menaker.
pages cm
ISBN 978-0-547-79423-5 (hardback) ISBN 978-0-544-33453-3 (paperback)
1. Menaker, Daniel. 2. Editors — United States — Biography.
3. Book editors — United States — Biography. I. Title.
PN149.9.M42A3 2013
070.4'1092 — dc23
2013019213

Book design by Melissa Lotfy

Printed in the United States of America
DOC 10 9 8 7 6 5 4 3 2 1

In significantly different form, portions of this book originally appeared in
the *New York Times Book Review;* the *New York Times* Week in Review; the anthology *Brothers: 26 Stories of Love and Rivalry,* published by Jossey-Bass; and
the *Barnes & Noble Review.* The humor piece "Certain Questions in the History of the Party" originally appeared in *The New Yorker.*

I am grateful to the following people for permission to quote from un-
published correspondence: Alice Munro (letters), Wallace and Allen Shawn
(a note to me from their father, William Shawn), and Ellen Brodkey (a note
to me from her husband, Harold Brodkey).

The names of some individuals in this book have been changed, out of
respect for their privacy.

Contents

Introduction

MY GODFATHER INVESTIGATED my father for the FBI and was involved in a car chase with Baby Face Nelson. My uncle had "Frederick Engels" for first and middle names. My father went to Mexico and spied on Trotsky for the Communist Party of the United States. My father's forebears were, according to an Orthodox Jewish camera dealer on West 45th Street, an important clan of Talmudic rabbis descended from King Solomon. (The man asked me if I was Jewish, and I said "Half," and he said "Your mother?," and I said "My father, pretty obviously," and he sort of waved away my claim to Jewishness, and I said, "It would have been good enough for Hitler.") My mother was an editor at *Fortune* when few women were editors. She could trace her lineage to William the Conqueror—if she cared about that kind of thing, which she didn't—and helped to establish the Newspaper Guild at Time, Inc. I attended the most prominent progressive ("Commugressive" was the neologism of a contemporary right-wing screed) private school in the United States, the aptronymic Little Red School House, on Bleecker Street in Greenwich Village, during the 1940s, when Leadbelly and the Weavers were singing at the Village Vanguard. Another of my uncles, Peter Lavrov Menaker, owned a leftist boys' camp in the Berkshires attended by William Gaines, founder of *Mad* magazine, and Victor Navasky, Publisher of *The Nation*, with a camp song written by its music counselor, Frank Loesser, the composer of the music and lyrics for *Guys and*

Dolls. I was taught to play the guitar by one of the sons of Julius and Ethel Rosenberg. I captained Swarthmore College's varsity soccer team to a 2–7–1 record, and I bought the first Bob Dylan album right when it came out because I thought the musician was a Welsh folksinger. My mistake, but a good one.

My brother died when he was twenty-nine after surgery for an injury that I caused.

I worked for twenty-six years in the brilliant crazy house called *The New Yorker*—where a man stood in the middle of the hall and said, loudly, "I am the greatest metropolitan reporter alive"; where a film critic regularly passed out drunk during movie screenings; where the Editor, William Shawn, a kind of genius, fell psychological prey to three or four short women who managed to get their hooks into him; where one of the cartoonists did his laundry in the men's room; where the succession politics that swirled around Shawn rivaled those of the papal succession in the eleventh century; where one of those successors, a smart, incredibly hard-working, but dizzy person, asked me if Jews would throw bagels at her if the magazine published an Art Spiegelman cover showing a Hassid kissing a black woman. She said I was the only Jewish editor she could find in the office.

I went on to work for fifteen years in book publishing, where my first boss, the husband of the potential bagel target, kept exhorting me to "eat like a moonkey." I also acquired a novel, *Everyone's Gone to the Moon,* by Philip Norman, about British journalism, which portrayed that (fictionalized) same boss in unflattering terms—acquired it because, as the boss put it, "I wouldn't want anyone else to pooblish this book, would I?" Hold your enemies close.

Later on, I made an offer for a book that I knew was too low in order to avoid working a second time with the writer in question, because he *could not stop talking.* I dreamed up the title *Primary Colors.*

Finally, Introduction-wise, I was diagnosed with lung cancer at the age of sixty-six and had a lobectomy and then a recurrence of the cancer in the remainder of my left lung. I have been treated with chemotherapy and futuristic radiation therapy and have just now had my fourth "clean" CT scan as I write this very sentence. The cancer led me to consider writing this book and in that way take stock of my life—at least my childhood and youth and professional life—and try to make sense of it. This latest scan has re-introduced me to a cancer patient's best friend: NED. No Evidence of Disease. But there's no telling how long he'll be hanging out around here. "Scan-to-scan anxiety is real," my oncologist told me. "Thanks, Doc," I said to myself.

Cancer can, at least for a while, have some benefits. It allows you to dodge onerous commitments. It strengthens friendships. It prevents you from taking good things for granted. It increases the urgency of parts of your life and shows up the trivialities. It requires you to find your courage.

Part I

No Television; Vitalis

Three months

(As told by Theareatha Rogowski, who took care of me and my brother, Mike, three years older, while my mother worked at *Fortune* magazine and my father worked, usually fecklessly, as an exporter.)

Danny, you was so sick. You couldn't keep anything down. Or it would be the other end. You looked like a little bunch of sticks with a bellybutton. They had to take you to the hospital. Your father said to me, "Readie, say goodbye to Danny. You won't be seeing him again." But I knew you was going to be all right. I just went and prayed that you would be all right and I knew you would be, but you was in that hospital for two months. We couldn't even visit you for more than an hour each day. That's the way it was back then.

Two and a half

I am playing in the driveway of my uncle Enge's house in New Marlborough, Massachusetts. My father, Robert Owen Menaker, is the youngest of seven. His siblings are George Menaker (no middle name), Frederick Engels Menaker (Uncle Enge—"rhymes with mange," he likes to say), William Morris Menaker, Peter Lavrov Menaker, Nicholas Chernechevsky Menaker, and Leonard Aveling Menaker. Their parents, Solomon and Fannie Menaker, came from Vilna and Odessa. They never married, out of a conviction that marriage was a form of oppression by the state. (More than half a century later, among Uncle Enge's papers, I was to find an essay about my grandfather by a visitor to his textile plant. "I know not what exact philosophy this gentleman of the people follows, but he treats those who toil in his factory with the greatest respect and financial rectitude," the visitor wrote. "There can be no doubt that he is a man of the people, and the fire of Revolution burns in his eyes.")

Enge owns a Guest Camp on Lake Buel, a few miles from his farmhouse. It's mainly for parents of the boys who go to Uncle Pete's camp, To-Ho-Ne, just north of the Guest Camp. To-Ho-Ne is the camp's Native American name. It means "Here will we camp."

The driveway of the farmhouse. It's summer, and Uncle Enge's rust-colored Chow-mix, Timmy, is looking out for me. I'm sitting on his back, pouring dirt and gravel over his head from a small tin bucket. I see a car go by slowly and pull into the grass parking area across the road from the house. A nice-looking man with wavy gray-and-brown hair gets out, crosses the road, and starts up the driveway.

He stops in front of me. "Where is your father, little boy?" the man asks me.

"In Souse America," I am said to have said. (I clearly recall the moment but not the content of the dialogue; my parents will tell me about it later—many times, and with amusement.)

"Really? Are you sure?"

"Yes. He's twavelin."

"Why isn't he here?"

"He's workin."

"Are you sure he isn't here?"

"Wait!" I say. "*You* are my father."

Four

Joe is mixing cement for my uncle in the farmhouse driveway. He's pouring water from a bucket into a tub. Joe is Joe Rogowski, a Polish immigrant laborer with almost incomprehensible English, who works for Enge in the summer and has taken a liking to Readie, who watches out for me and Mike up here while my parents stay in New York. They visit on weekends. How Joe landed here I have no idea. He leaves the tub of cement for a few minutes, and my brother, Mike, seven, tells me I can help Joe by picking up the bucket and pouring more water into the cement mix. I do that. Joe comes back, gets furious, and spanks me — the first and last time I have ever been spanked. Readie is very angry at him. "Don't you *ever* hit my baby, Joseph Whateveryournameis," she says.

Even while I am being spanked, and am crying, I am fascinated by the two half-fingers on Joe's right hand. He cut the other halves off while using a power saw.

Later, Joe is sitting on the porch while my uncle and some friends are talking about traveling. My uncle says, "It's true that the last mile home is the longest. When I get to the train station in Great Barrington, it seems to take forever to get up here to the farm. And then there's so much work to do when I get here."

"No such ting wongis mywis," Joe says.

"What are you saying, Joe?" Enge says.

"I say no such ting wongis mywis."

This continues to be a puzzlement. Enge asks him again what he's trying to say.

"You say wast my to chouse is wongis. No such ting wongis mywis."

Ah! No such thing as longest miles. Quite right. But the real understanding—what I know now, at seventy-two—is how unusual it was for Joe, the handyman, to sit in on our discussions. He felt welcome. He was welcome. Enge has told me that my grandfather Solomon, who for a while ran a textile factory in New Jersey on Socialist principles, always had workers at the family table. The Workmen's Circle awarded him a trophy cup, which sits on a shelf in my uncle's house, which will, many years in the future, be my house.

My parents send my brother and me up here to the country with Readie to escape the polio epidemics in the city and also, as I will learn later, so that they can live it up. At the end of this particular summer, I go home to Barrow Street, in Greenwich Village, and I see footprints on the ceiling. I ask my father whose they are, and he says, "Your mother's." I ask how they got there, and he says, "When your mother has a little too much to drink, she can fly."

Every summer is absolutely enchanted, endless—until it ends.

In New York, I've learned to turn the dial on the veneered wooden boxy radio we have—a dial set against a lit-up, canvas-colored rhomboid—and one Saturday morning, I find a station in New Jersey, WAAT, that plays an hour of country music. I discover T. Texas Tyler and Ernest Tubb and Kitty Wells and Roy Acuff and of course Hank Williams. My mother comes into the living room one morning and finds me sitting on the floor listening to Ernest Tubb—probably "Soldier's Last Letter." "What on earth is that caterwauling?" she says. She says it not in true horror but with her characteristic demure bemusement. She also sincerely wants an answer. WAAT broadcasts a polka hour before the country-music program, and I like that, too—it seems equally "real" in a way that I can't then understand. But it also sounds pretty watery next to "Blood on the Saddle."

Five

In the "Fives" at the Little Red School House, the very progressive private school on Bleecker Street in Greenwich Village, a new boy arrives. Walter Brooks. He's black and can sing "Cincinnati's Dancing Pig" well. When I get home from school, my mother asks me if Walter has arrived. I say yes. She says, "He's the Negro boy, I think." I say, "I don't know. I forget." Many years later, it occurs to me that our teachers' asking Walter to sing "Cincinnati's Dancing Pig" from time to time smacked a little of minstrelsy.

Little Red is in fact filled with Little Reds. Our Principal, Randolph Smith, comes close to being subpoenaed by the House Un-American Activities Committee. Or he actually is subpoenaed. The kids from the parochial school on the southwest corner of Bleecker and Sixth Avenue throw fluorescent light bulbs at us as we march to and from the playground around the corner on Houston Street. They are hoping to kill us with the poison gas said to be inside the bulbs.

Seven

As we march to and from the playground in the fall of 1948, we live up to the parochial-school kids' worst opinion of us by chanting a chant for Henry Wallace for President—a chant we seem to know osmotically, from the pink air we all breathe. It goes something like this:

Dewey is in the outhouse crying like a baby.
Truman is in the doghouse, barking like crazy.
Wallace is in the White House, talking to a lady.

Eight to twelve

Every summer at Enge's Guest Camp a truck drives around the long circular driveway and along the paths that lead from one cabin to another blasting out a fog of DDT, a common anti-mosquito practice. Some other kids and I run through the fog for the fun of disappearing and reappearing. We try not to breathe the stuff in, but we don't try all that hard. Is it this—or the cigarette smoking all around me and then *by* me; or the city air, which leaves particulate soot on our windowsills in New York; or the exhaust from cars and trucks when, almost twenty years later, I spend two summers as a toll taker on the New York State Thruway; or bad luck; or punishment for my sins—that I started paying for at sixty-six, when I was first diagnosed with lung cancer? One man at the Guest Camp, a financial guy of some kind, plays gin rummy all day under a plume of smoke from the monstrous cigar he keeps plugged in his mouth. He has a constant tic of moving it back and forth, from one side to the other, like a horizontal windshield wiper. Sometime later, he is sent to jail for embezzlement.

There is a zinc icebox beside and below the raised back porch of the Guest Camp's lodge, which overlooks the lake. Once a week or so in the summer, an ice truck delivers two huge slabs of ice—five feet by three feet by one foot—that the driver and Enge's waiters wrestle into the box with gigantic black tongs. Like a monster's two snaggled incisors. At the bottom of the icebox is a drain for the runoff. The men release the first slab a foot or so above the bottom of the icebox, and the impact of ice on zinc sounds mortal. Enge and the cook and the waiters store some perishable food in there. You open the top of the icebox by means of a rope and pulley, and there is butter and bacon and beef and broccoli. If I jump up and grab the rope high enough, it lifts me off the porch as the top goes down. I am that skinny, from that early illness. That's what Dr. Mandel says.

An Italian guy who drives a fruit-and-vegetable truck around to the various camps and resorts on the lake pulls into the circular driveway behind the lodge once a week or so. He holds up a plum and says, "It's-a beautiful, Engie—juss-a like-a youself." Enge is in fact ugly, in a handsome way. Short, slender, with a large bald head (baldness from exposure to mustard gas in the First World War, he tells me) and very big ears and quite a nose— he resembles some portraits and statues of Cervantes and even more closely some images of Cervantes's creation, Don Quixote. And Gandhi.

On weekends Enge calls square dances in the lodge. He sits in a chair on top of a table with a primitive microphone and speakers that carry his voice around the big room. *I* put the chair on the table. *I* turn the amplifier on. *I* manfully hand Enge's accordion up to him. *I* know that he will call out "Four couples! Four couples!" to start things off. *I* know all the steps and dances— the allemandes, the do-si-dos, the grand right-and-lefts. *I* know gents to the center and break 'er down. *I* help new dancers when they get tangled up in complicated figures. *I* know how to swing my partner, usually three or four times my age, with one hand on her shoulder, one of her hands on my shoulder, and our other two hands clasped under the bridge. *I* know that at the end of a set, Enge is going to sing, slightly suggestively, "Take her out, you know where. / Take her out and give her air." Sixty people or more dance on weekend nights. Sometimes there are squares in the card room and library, off the big room. Sometimes there is a game of Rock Crusher (oh, I know what that means), a form of high-low poker, going on at a table in the corner of the big room. Sometimes a CPA guest is adding columns of figures at that same table in between hands, amid the din and dancing, adding them so fast—running a pencil down the columns almost as fast as he would be if he were just crossing them out—that I can't believe it.

The guests are mainly Jewish, the sons and daughters or grandsons and granddaughters of immigrants from Eastern Europe. Their names are Mishkin, Goldberg, Leonard, Friedman, Cohen. They are doctors and lawyers and accountants and garment-industry types and schoolteachers. Moving up very fast, many have left their Brooklyn accents behind, but they're always dropping Yiddish words and phrases into their conversation, the most exotic, to me, being something that sounds like *machataynista*— which evidently denotes what an in-law on one side of a married couple is to an in-law on the other. A husband's brother's wife, say, to a wife's sister's husband. These Jews—so complicated. When my WASPy cousins from my mother's side of the family— my Aunt Priscilla Grace and her children—drive over from Milton, near Boston, to visit, they seem a different species altogether, with their Brahmin accents, untroubled brows, and apparent lack of complexities. (Later, I learn that they have their own problems, of course.) The guests have a wonderful time in this very basic camp setting, dancing, swimming, canoeing, drinking (before dinner; no alcohol at the tables on the long porch), going to Tanglewood to hear the Boston Symphony Orchestra, to Jacob's Pillow for the dance festival.

I get to go back up to the farmhouse with Readie and sleep in the back room over the kitchen. Mike and I take our .22 rifles into the woods and shoot at birds and squirrels. We sit at the "family table." We swim for hours on end, playing water tag with the white float as a safe base. We are privileged and doted upon, partly because many guests want to get closer to my uncle, who is so charismatic and sociable. I get to lie on the lawn at the farmhouse and wait for the mailman to deliver the previous day's New York Times, which has the baseball box scores from two and even three days before that, so that reading them is like time travel. I live in the Yankees' past.

Do you believe—or remember? There was no television. So what was there? Charades, Scrabble, poker, canasta, gin rummy, backgammon, parlor games of all kinds, at camp and at the farmhouse. Someone who doesn't know the game goes out of the room for a few minutes, and Enge gives us The Principle: We're all to answer yes-or-no questions as if we're the person to our left. I always try to have a woman on my left. Enge has written two small Sentinel paperbacks about such party games: "72 Surefire Ways of Having Fun" and "The Life of the Party: 67 Ways to Have Fun." That's 139 ways to have fun. And we sing. Camp songs, union songs, songs from the Spanish Civil War—"Freiheit!" is my favorite—American folksongs of all kinds. And Enge begins to teach me to play the guitar. And conversation—so much talking, arguing, laughter. At home in the Village, when I am nine or ten, we rent a television set for a week or so to watch the World Series. It's almost as big as a refrigerator and has a black-and-white screen the size of a Chiclet. That's it for TV.

Friends and relations surround me and Mike, in the country and in the city. The dinner table at the farmhouse and in the Village, especially during the autumn, often has ten or fifteen people sitting around it—uncles, cousins, friends—all declaiming and arguing, usually about politics, with loud denunciations of government and capitalism. This is where I learn my deep and nearly reflexive distrust of those in positions of power. The fine points of doctrine escape me, but generally: You can't trust them.

Despite a kind of built-in anxiety, almost surely the legacy of that same early-infancy, largely isolated hospital stay, I find the world enchanting, thick with point-making and sensations and love, love especially from Readie. Readie says to Enge no, she can't do work for him and look out for me and Mike at the same time. "He has some nerve, that man," she says when he tells her to hang his laundry on the clothesline behind the house. "Your uncle is a trying case and a case to be tried," she says. "Just because I'm black!" When the sheets are on the line, I run between them, inhaling sunshine and Tide and imagining that these are a ship's sails. When we're a little older, Readie takes on the care of the child of one of her sisters who can't care for him herself. He is two or three, and his name is Raymond, and now he comes up to the farmhouse with us, and my brother and I regard him as a sort of mascot.

If I make coffee for Readie, she says, "I want it black, just like me. But you don't have to make it. Slavery days are over. Someone just ought to tell your uncle. He don't seem to know."

How Readie got to us I don't know. She was born in South Carolina, had many half-brothers and half-sisters, ate clay when she was little, she was so hungry, and picked cotton along with the rest of her family. She can barely write. Where she got her enormous warmth and affection and good sense from I also don't know, but I'm grateful for it in my mind every day, including this minute, at seventy-two, sitting once again in the farmhouse, when the memory of being able to so completely count on her makes me feel safe, protected by her love and vigilance, no matter what comes next.

If this picture of Readie bears a close resemblance to Faulkner's Dilsey and other, similar literary black nannies, there's no help for it. For this is what she is like, at least for Mike and me. As we all grow older, I will come to appreciate her for her robust humor and her keen insights into the ways my family worked and didn't work and her iron will about controlling — and refusing to dwell on — her diabetes. And then I will see, sadly, that she is becoming a hoarder in her small public-housing apartment in Chelsea, perhaps owing to her poverty-stricken childhood. But as children, Mike and I regard her as the safest refuge from our troubles and a sensible check on our bad behavior.

So I had two mothers. My mother and Readie. Readie called me and Mike "my babies." She had, essentially, adopted us, as she adopted Raymond. And as my wife and I were later to adopt two children, our cynosures. I had two fathers, too. Well, three, actually. My father taught me to drive — lessons continued later by my brother — but usually, because of his handsome and charming immaturity, he sat in the back seat of my family much of the time. He may have worked better in the world than I knew, or know, but I didn't, and don't, know it. He was a nice guy. Drank a little too much, and when he did so, sometimes, mortifyingly, offered back rubs to my and my brother's girlfriends. Lived in my mother's shadow, dwelled on his failures. But still a charming and often spontaneous person. Then there was Enge, who began teaching me guitar, taught me square dancing, games, a little Yiddish, how to bid for eggs at a farmer's auction in Hillsdale, how to oil a rifle, how to make blintzes, how to oil a wood floor, how to tell a story. Then there was Mike, who provided me with some of the guidance and sternness I needed at home. There will be more fathers in my life.

I think that some of us have more than one mother and many if not most of us, especially boys, have more than one father.

Nine

From time to time, I see protectiveness underneath Mike's bullying, as when a friend and I spend a little too much time in the bathroom together and Mike figures out what's going on in there and puts a stop to it. He needn't have worried—I am passive and basically uninterested. Obliging. But he is looking out for me. He and Readie.

With my great but hidden anxiety, I take the train by myself from Great Barrington to New York—to Grand Central Terminal, in the middle of the summer. I have a dentist appointment in the city. My father will meet me at the information booth at Grand Central. The train comes in on the lower level. I wait at the small information booth there, while, as it turns out, my father is waiting for me at the main booth on the main level.

No one shows up. I feel panicky and cold and sweaty. Where is he? Fifteen minutes go by. Trembling, I find a cop and tell him the situation. He asks if I know my family's home phone number. CHelsea 2-4685. He calls and my mother answers. Somehow it's all worked out, and the cop takes me up the wide stairs to where my father is still waiting. He apologizes to me for the confusion, and I begin to calm down, but he also finds it surprising that I was so frightened. "Did you really think I had abandoned you?" he asks. Again, the bemusement, and a sense that my brother and I are perhaps less cherished than provided for, but this is at least partly the style—almost the vogue—in middle-class parenting of the Forties.

Ten

My brother and I are always fighting—"roughhousing," my parents call it. Mike beats me up a lot. I spend much of the year in a headlock. But I am a genius teaser, an unremitting critic of his asthma and flat feet.

We cut the heads off wooden matches and then use a wire cutter to snip off the heads of pins. We force the blunt end of the pins into one end of the matches, use an X-acto knife to put slits in the other end, put paper "fins" in the slits, and then hurl these tiny missiles at each other. When thrown correctly, the pinpoints go through clothes and sting the target nicely. We have a rule: No aiming above the shoulders. My mother discovers us at this sport, is horrified, and forbids us to ever play it again.

I don't know if our rivalry is unusually intense, but it is *our* rivalry, and I can't imagine any other brothers' competition being fiercer. It is like a project, an enterprise that we feel obliged to sustain. We are, after all, competing for the greatest prize in the history of the world—our mother's love and attention.

Despite the sibling mayhem, I feel safe at home on West 4th Street. I can go about the city, or at least the Village, alone, but if I go more than three blocks away and find myself in a place I don't recognize, a blanket of cold terror begins to settle around me, and I retreat.

And when the family drives to Uncle Enge's house in the country together, my father and brother sit in the front seat and begin talking about being lost, to tease me, but I don't know they are teasing—they fool me every time—and that same cold terror comes over me. They can't have any idea how cruel this is.

And there is terror of an abstract kind: arithmetic books. 6+3 was easy. 6+7. Doable. 58+174. I could handle that. But farther ahead in this year's arithmetic book impossibilities lurk. Multiplication, long division, and especially division in which the number outside the house is bigger than the number inside the house. How can that possibly make sense? Mike shows me his math book; it has problems that look like division with nothing at all outside the house—just a V with a bar extending to the right and a number underneath. "Square roots," Mike says. "You'll never be able to understand them, because you're an idiot."

Near our brownstone on West 4th is a movie theater that all

the kids in the neighborhood call The Dump. I won't go there without my brother, but when we do go, it is a wild kind of fun. The Dump shows W. C. Fields shorts, Buck Rogers serials, cheesy Western features. It *is* a dump. It is mayhem in there. Almost all boys. Kids shout out curses, throw soda at each other, get into fights. The management seems not to care. Maybe there is no management — maybe someone has designed The Dump as a cave of childhood disinhibition. The admission price is seven cents. By some group unconscious agreement, you get a nickel from your parents and beg the other two cents from passers-by: arithmetic in action.

My school report from Little Red says what it has always said, from kindergarten on: There is some praise of my intelligence and abilities but it's followed by something like, "Danny is an anxious child who continues to prefer fantasy play to organized games and sports. He is preoccupied with being 'right' all the time, which makes his insecurity all the more evident."

In fourth and fifth grades I have a titanic crush on a blond girl, one of the few non-Jews in the class (thus beginning a romantic pattern for my Oedipal half-Jewish self). She is the daughter of a respected actress. I try to sit next to her in class, and she looks at me with distaste and moves away. But one day, when we are playing Spin the Bottle in someone's apartment, I spin the bottle and it points at her. She's clearly exasperated but says, "Come on," and leads me to the small bedroom where everyone closes the door and kisses — or pretends to, as I am sure is going to happen now. But no. She says, "Do you want to do this right?" I stammer something and she pushes me down on the bed and lies on top of me and kisses me and moves her hips against me. Then she says we have to go back, leaving me close to comatose with pleasure and bafflement, and a cigarillo erection.

Eleven

We've moved from the Village to Nyack, New York, two-fifths small-town white Protestants, two-fifths recent immigrant families and "ethnic"—blacks, Italians, Irish—one-fifth Wonder Bread commuters. My parents can no longer afford the tuition at Little Red. I am in sixth grade at the Liberty Street School, and how could it be more different from Little Red? It couldn't. Desks in rows? No circles of chairs for discussion? *Grades*? A black kid saying to me, "Give me yo lunch money, white boy"? Bullying of every other kind? Lunch money itself? Fierce Darwinism on the playground. Softball with no gloves? The word "nigger"? A girl who "likes" me? Jeannie—she's cute. Wait! Another one! Katie—very blond, very pretty. They're friends. They want me to go with them to the movies up on Main Street on Saturday. They buy me popcorn. They both hold hands with me.

Mrs. Delaney, my teacher, and her husband are visiting my family for dinner. (We live in a white stucco house across from a convent, with a fine view of the Hudson River.) Mrs. Delaney makes it clear that she is Anglo-Irish rather than Irish-Irish. She says to my parents in her soft, semi-Southern accent, "It's so good to have Danny in our class—a real American boy."

"American?" my mother says.

"Well, I mean a real American. Not Italian or Greek or anything like that. And then there are all the Negroes."

In fact, although my mother is indeed a "real American"—Mary Randolph Grace, descended from the aforementioned William the Conqueror (according to a silly, self-published vanity book, *Fitz Randolph Traditions,* written by a maiden aunt)—she helped found the Newspaper Guild. And my brother, Michael Grace Menaker, and I are the "real-American" half-Jewish atheist sons of a father who is or at least was a member of the Communist Party and whose own parents never married, and whose last name is a corruption of the Hebrew name of a clan of rabbis. Neighbors in Nyack have complained of my bringing Negroes home to play with after school. One of them, Maurice, is too old and big for sixth grade, but he serves as my bodyguard against the bullies who have threatened me as a matter of routine.

The one thing that seems to bother Mrs. Delaney about me is that I am the only boy in the class who has long hair—that is, who doesn't have a crewcut. One day, she calls me up to the front of the room and asks me to sit in a chair facing the other kids. She starts to braid my hair. Everybody laughs and I duck away from her and go back to my desk. Not only do I not mind what has just happened, I enjoy it.

One of the first questions other kids in Nyack ask me is "What church do you go to?" I have never known anyone who went to church or even to synagogue except my New York dentist, Dr. M. Joel Friedman. He once invited my family to Passover and I had to read a passage from whatever it is that you read from. I had made my parents swear that I wouldn't have to read. But I did have to. There were maybe forty people spread across two adjoining rooms, and each reader used a microphone. When it was my turn, instead of "the sacred hand of Israel," I read "the scared hand of Israel," and everyone laughed. I was humiliated.

In Nyack, I don't care to talk about my half-Jewishness when asked the unprecedented church question. There are only two or three Jewish kids in my class, as opposed to the ninety per cent at Little Red, and they and their families keep somewhat to themselves. I have never met anyone who goes to the Methodist church, so I say "Methodist." My mistake. This satisfies my inter-rogators for a while. But later on, when I am best friends with the son of the Dutch Reformed minister (I steal money from his fami-ly's house when they are away), my friends find out that my claim to churchgoing Methodism isn't true. I'm in tight enough by then to survive this mendacity.

It's recess, and while running around the playground at the Lib-erty Street School, I fall and break my arm. I'm taken to Nyack Hospital and my parents show up and I have surgery to set my arm. Sometime later I find myself lying up in the air, looking down at my body in a hospital bed and at my parents and my brother, who is fourteen, gathered around the bed. Above me, the ceil-ing dematerializes and I turn my head around to see—I swear to you—a great white light, forming a tunnel, leading up and away into a glorious realm of existence far superior to the one below me. I can see indistinct figures within the light, and they are beck-oning me in dulcet tones to join them. It's tempting, but some-how I understand that it isn't time to go there yet. So I turn myself over in mid-air, so that I am floating on my back, and I slowly and reluctantly descend toward the bed. I fit perfectly into my body, and I wake up. For the first time I can remember, I feel great hap-piness and great sadness at the same time. How can that be?

Thirteen

At Uncle Enge's Guest Camp, I am the waiter for the children's table. These are the kids too young to go to the boys' camp. Or they're girls. I steal change from the little cup in the top drawer of the desk in the business office of the lodge and take it down the road to Gibson's Grove. I buy ice cream and candy and play pinball. The jukebox on the porch overlooking the lake sends Kay Starr's "Wheel of Fortune" out over the water day and night — you can hear it everywhere.

My uncle's partner, Glen, runs the business part of the Guest Camp. That he and Enge are a gay couple I won't realize for another year or two. Glen is tall and slender, from the Midwest, mild, pleasant, droll. He sings solos for the choir of the Methodist church in Great Barrington. I learn dozens of hymns from listening to him sing in the farmhouse, accompanied by Enge on the piano. "Beulah Land," "What a Friend We Have in Jesus," "In the Garden." This last always makes me laugh, because a part of the first verse goes, "And the voice I hear / Falling on my ear / The Son of God discloses." How Glen fetched up here I (once again) don't know. Later, when I am fifteen or so, a local teenager whom Enge has fired from his summer job accuses Enge and Glen of homosexuality. He says he has seen them having sex in their bedroom. State troopers pull up in the driveway. Charges are brought, and there is a trial. Enge's lawyer is Tom McDade, the ex-FBI man, now comptroller of General Foods, who has gotten to know my family because he was a counselor at Pete's camp for a few summers. Tom took a liking to my whole family, kept my father and Enge out of trouble with the House Un-American Activities Committee, built a house nearby, and was godfather to Mike and me.

I don't attend the trial but am told that Tom asked the kid on the witness stand exactly how it was that he saw the act. The kid stumbled around. Tom asked if it was through the keyhole of their bedroom door. The kid said, "Yes! That was it." Tom said, "But there is no keyhole in that door." The judge dismissed the case.

I organize an "army" of the children I wait on, and we use sticks for guns and go on "raids" on the adults' cabins — no doubt often when they are taking a nap or trying to have sex. I love ordering the kids around, a nascent will to power that I never come to attain fully as an adult; it remains largely a matter of fantasy because I don't have the guile—or the temporary, conniving obsequiousness, or the genuine authority—necessary to get all the way up there. I will come close, though. Not bad. In my thirties and forties, I will begin to learn to hold down the insecure tyrant more securely, kowtow more, strategize, triangulate, navigate. It will always make me queasy, but it works, doesn't it? And it's necessary.

My "soldiers" at the Guest Camp desert, because young as they are, they get that I'm playing this game largely to boss them around. Same happened at Little Red, where I organized a "gang" on the playground. They all defected after a few weeks, and I was left to fume and wonder why.

Fourteen

I am sitting at the kitchen counter in our house in South Nyack. My mother arrives home from her arduous commute to the offices of *Fortune,* where she has become a legendary copy editor—an expert on grammar, usage, idiom. She was a Classics major at Bryn Mawr and knows Greek and Latin. She is beautiful—she always wears her brown hair in a bun, always acts in a somewhat flirtatious way, even with Mike and me, always makes an impression of effortless good looks. She says to me, "When I got off the bus I heard one Negro boy on a bicycle say to another, who wanted a ride, 'Get the fuck up on the bicycle.'"

I have never heard her use this word before. She says, "I wonder what part of speech 'the fuck' is in that sentence structure."

She has already threatened to disown me if she ever hears me say "Tiffany's" again—instead of "Tiffany."

Another evening, around the same time, she tells my father and brother and me, at dinner, of a researcher who burst into tears when she jokingly said to her that day, about a question of factual accuracy, "Let me know when you make up your alleged mind." My mother asks, "Isn't it clear that I was just kidding?" Before she dies, suffering from metastatic pancreatic cancer, forty years later, she writes a last entry in her journal: "Is this what I get for feeling so superior my entire life?"

Mrs. Giles, my ninth-grade English teacher, assigns us homework of writing sentences that are declarative, compound, complex, interrogative, and imperative, and one sentence in the passive voice. I write:

> *"The dog chased the cat."*
> *"The dog chased the cat, and then the cat chased the dog."*
> *"After the dog chased the cat, the cat chased the dog."*
> *"Did the dog chase the cat?"*
> *"Dog, chase the cat!"*
> And, of course: *"The cat was chased by the dog."*

She says it's very funny and gives me a C. *What? A C?* But it is the beginning of my humor-writing career.

Fourteen to twenty-one

In Nyack, The Boys play sports, get into small amounts of trouble with the cops, find bars that allow us to pretend to be eighteen. Peruna's in Spring Valley, the Deer Head in Blauvelt, but mainly the wonderful bar owned first by Charlie and called Charlie's, and then, when Charlie's bartender Paul O'Donoghue takes over the business, O'Donoghue's. When I'm home from college, and when

Paul gets a little tipsy himself and starts talking with a brogue and calling out "Up the Irish!," I sometimes get to tend bar, at two or so in the morning and after the place has been locked up and only The Boys and a few stragglers—like the closeted doctor who once treated me for groinal ringworm with a little too much interest and the high-school Latin teacher, Stan Callahan, the good Callahan, grizzled, portly—remain. (There was also a bad Callahan teaching at Liberty Street. I stole the key ring from his desk and threw it away. Everyone hated him.) I sometimes run into my brother at O'Donoghue's and am proud to be seen with him, as he was one of The Boys in his class.

Mainly, for both of us, Nyack High School is "American Graffiti East." There are sports and friends and Fifties clothes, like white bucks and argyle socks and white shirts and khakis and at one point chartreuse shoelaces, and for the girls sack dresses, girdles, white blouses, and circle pins, and there are romances and diabolically unique bra clasps and soccer and baseball practice and loud-muffler cars that break down all the time and "marriage manuals" left in bookshelves for adolescents to read and pickup basketball games in the freezing cold, when your hands start out like slabs of ice and magically end up as warm as waffles and tingle when you go indoors, and the mesmerizing Army-McCarthy hearings on television sets that show test patterns in the mornings and summer jobs as park attendants and the blunt truths, for middle-class white kids, of "race music" and then the rest of early rock and roll, which seems so impossibly innocent now, and dancing the lindy—yes, the lindy—for hours at parties. My girlfriend Pam, who when we graduate is voted Wittiest, is the daughter of the man who drives the bus that my parents take to their jobs in New York.

Mike is cool. Six feet two, black hair, very white teeth, handsome, smart. On the swimming team. He works construction one summer—he's a hod carrier—and at the end of August he is Mediterraneanly tan and has put on ten pounds of muscle. He has good girlfriends—one especially good one thinks I'm cute and kisses me—and he drinks as much as he should, as much as we all do, with our class rings turned around at Peruna's so that they look to the bartender like wedding bands, we hope. The drinking age is eighteen, so kids from neighboring New Jersey, where it is twenty-one, cross the state line to drink and get into fights with us.

For all the fun, I continue to be anxious and timid, at least outside familiar circumstances, but Mike takes care of some part of that after I get to Nyack. He makes me go out for sports by not allowing me into the house after school. He takes over from my father in teaching me how to drive and sees to it that I fit in. He still makes terrific fun of me. My hair is thick and, to my shame, curly verging on kinky, and I am always trying to straighten it, with the aid of Brylcreem or Vitalis. One day, when I'm about to go somewhere with him in his '49 Plymouth with Duotone mufflers and I ask him to wait because I have to comb my hair, he says, "Your what?" And from then on, to him, my hair is my "what," as in, "Get a whatcut—your what's too long." But I often get the better of him in the taunting that goes on between us—I am quicker and sharper with words. I set the gold standard for ridiculous, devastating insults when, after he has punched me in the arm, leaving it close to paralyzed, and called me a "blivet" for taking a long time in the shower, I look at him with his towel wrapped around his waist and say, "At least I don't have Jewish nipples." He looks down at his chest with concern and goes to find our mother to ask her if what I said was true.

Mike is always telling me, as I trail three grades behind him, how much harder school will be "next year," but I keep on outdoing him, at least partly because he keeps on challenging and goading me. So then he disdains me as an intellectual, even though I am also a pretty good athlete. But I can tell that he's also proud of me, especially after I get to college. My striving is not only to compete with him but to please him. His opinion of me means more than anyone else's. (Later, on the day before his wedding, we're playing pickup basketball outside his fiancée's house in New Jersey, and I make some semi-fancy move or other, and Mike stands back and says, "I can see I've taught you well, my boy.")

Younger brothers often idealize their older brothers, but Mike really is pretty remarkable. He is admired and praised in high school, and at Dartmouth he is rushed by Alpha Delta Phi, the crazy and wonderful fraternity that later becomes the basis for *Animal House,* and is beloved by his brothers there as well. Chris Miller, who wrote the screenplay for *Animal House,* is a Dartmouth freshman when Mike is a senior. I actually know some of the real-life people whose nicknames the movie uses — Otter and Flounder, for example. There is a room under the attic stairs in Nyack that my mother names Flounder's Room, because Flounder — Nick Fate, a name I always wished I had — being far from his home in Oklahoma, sleeps off some of his Thanksgiving drunks there. My girlfriends always, but always, fall in love with Mike. He is smooth, funny, relaxed.

He and I talk to each other a lot about sex and other basic matters. He tells me about resorting one night, in the absence of something more conventional, to bacon grease. I tell him about sleeping with a girl who, once she is interested and involved in what is going on, can have an orgasm from simply being ordered emphatically enough to have one. He tells me about a prostitute he unwittingly picked up in Copenhagen who was obsessed with

Buddy Holly and, to his shock, gave him a squirting demonstra-
tion of lactation. On long-distance car trips we don't stop to use
gas-station bathrooms but piss in the beer cans we've just emp-
tied—and then marvel at how warm piss is. We practice flatu-
lence as a second language.

For all these and other mild delinquencies, at Dartmouth,
where he careens around the Northeast on "road trips" to wom-
en's colleges, betting his life against alcohol and sleep, Mike becomes more and more conservative, in reaction to our family's radical background and as a result of hanging around with
kids much richer than we are. He wants us to put "estate lights"
around the house in Nyack and is embarrassed that the windows
don't have beautiful curtains. In law school and for a little while
afterward, he supports the Vietnam War, which makes my parents and me both angry and sad. Eventually, though, he changes
his mind, no doubt partly because of the strong views of his girlfriend, who works for a nonprofit agency. He seems to be headed
toward the liberal fold—the fold into which most children of the
mid-century Socialists and Communists my family know have
folded themselves. He never gets all the way there.

Fifteen

My biology teacher, Mr. Z., asks the class if anyone knows the
name of the bush that has yellow flowers early in the spring. I
raise my hand, am called on, and say, "Forsythia." A few minutes
later, when the class ends, Mr. Z. asks me to stay behind for a minute. He says to me, "You know, it's a good thing that you know the
names of flowers and things like that, but you might want to keep
that kind of stuff to yourself." He adds: "You know."

"No," I say. "Why?"

"Well, because other kids might think you're a homosexual."

It will take me years to purge most of the racism and homophobia that I inhale in the Fifties at Nyack High School. I actively dislike myself for giving in to these and other bigotries—though it's true that my friends freely, relentlessly use such slurs against and among each other, along with insults (a lame white version of the Dozens) to each other's mothers and disparaging nicknames based on the way we look. My nickname for six years was "Schnoz."

Honestly? Vestiges of these hateful reflexes remain in me to this day, like a splinter or buckshot under the skin which never works its way out.

I steal 45s from the little record store in Nyack. The owner of the store follows me out the door one Saturday and grabs me by the shirt collar and drags me back inside and calls the police. A red-faced cop yells at me for half an hour. He asks me who else steals records. I give him the name of a bully—someone everybody detests. I doubt that he steals records. The cop then calls my parents. They come to pick me up, and they say nothing to me about this embarrassment except, from my mother, "This is very disappointing."

I never steal again. Well, I do. That summer, in the record store in Great Barrington, I steal the same record I had tried to steal in Nyack when I was caught. It is a two-disc Elvis Presley 45 album with four of his biggest hits, including "Blue Suede Shoes."

I soon learn that this is a cover of Carl Perkins's recording of the same song, the song he himself wrote—as Pat Boone covered Little Richard's "Tutti Frutti," hilariously, and the Crew Cuts covered the R&B hit "Sh-Boom" (with a little less self-embarrassment). This appropriation makes me indignant, now that I have gone straight, at least with regard to other people's property.

Sixteen

I get a summer job as a park attendant at Hook Mountain State Park, in Upper Nyack. The boss is a guy named John. He does the Jumble in the *New York Daily News* in thirty seconds flat. There is a park cop on duty here in the summer. He is a high-school teacher in a nearby town during the school year and is for some nutty reason allowed to carry a gun here at the park. A gun. In 1957. He keeps touching it, and once, when some picnickers disregard his barked order to clean up the lawn around them, puts his hand on the butt of his gun and says, "Don't make me use this."

My job is to clean out the toilets and pick up stray pieces of paper on the grass with one of those sticks with a nail on the end of it. Cleaning out the toilets: Better not to go into it, I think, as the toilets did not flush but needed to be flushed out with a hose. Never mind. The Dalit of Nyack, New York—that's me. Anyway, the park is on two levels—down by the Hudson River and high up on a kind of plateau—connected by a winding road. And when I'm supposed to be on litter patrol I often sit and relax on a big rock above that road, so that I can see when John is driving up and get up and get to "work" about ten seconds before he arrives. Sometimes I jog for a minute, in this direction or that, so as not to be in exactly the same place every time he reaches the top of the hill. A good deal of work to avoid work.

John calls me "Bob," because the legal name on my working papers is Robert D. Menaker. I feel like a different person when he calls me "Bob." I feel like—well, Bob.

Seventeen

A few months before graduating from Nyack High School, I am walking through the halls with my shirt untucked—against the rules. Doc Malinsky, the trainer for the athletic teams—a mean, small-eyed man with a belt-cantilevered belly—stops me in the hall.

"Tuck it in, Menaker."

"I'd rather not."

"I ought to punch you right in your fucking mouth, you fucking Communist."

A few weeks later, Doc Malinsky suddenly leaves town. He was caught blowing a junior with a perpetually maniacal grin in the training room. Jack Lawrence, the handsome baseball coach, Doc's friend, who wears colorful muscle T's and is married to a gargoyle of a woman, and the one who deliberately threw a hard pitch at me during batting practice one day, disappears with Doc.

Just before high-school graduation, I and a friend of mine—the guy whose house I stole money from when the family was away—sneak out at 2 a.m. with a can of green paint and two paintbrushes. We walk up to the high school, about a mile away, and paint our class number—'59—in six or seven different places on the outside of the building. The next morning, it elicits admiration from the high-school kids and outrage among teachers and the administration. I have an impulse to tell them that when we found an open window the night before, we went inside the building but, after talking it over, decided that vandalizing the interior would be going too far.

We are studying a poem in Dr. Roody's Advanced Placement senior English class. She asks us to say what the word "grace" brings to mind. I raise my hand and say something like "Being physically graceful."

"What else?" Dr. Roody says.

"Kindness or courtesy—like 'gracious,'" I say.

"Well, yes, in a way. Isn't there something else important?" I can't think of anything besides my mother's maiden name, Grace, but to mention that would bring some after-class derision from my classmates and probably a reprimand from Dr. Roody. I don't make my mistake.

"Not that I know of," I say.

"This is just one of the problems with people who don't go to church," Dr. Roody says.

When I go to Swarthmore College to be interviewed, the Admissions person asks me if I know where I rank in my high-school class. I almost say "Third"—which is what I tell other, less official adults if the subject comes up, or if I somehow manage to make it come up. But at the last second, I remember to tell the truth: "Fifth."

Does everyone tend to steal, cheat, and inflate this way, I wonder. What is wrong with me, I also wonder. I will never be able to answer that question fully, though I do later learn that my family's odd dynamics no doubt contributed to my dishonesties. I am talking about my parents' unequal marriage: my father's serious insecurities, my mother's psychologically seductive nature, her intellectual superiority. These dynamics lead me to shy away from real intimacy—especially after tragedy strikes—which in many cases will hurt others badly. I'm grateful that I don't seem to have passed such defects or emotional blockages on to my son and daughter, Will and Elizabeth. A little iconoclasm, yes. But certain symptoms of poor character which it has taken me a lifetime to try to repair? No. Knock wood.

When I apply to Swarthmore, I make my parents promise not to pull the one or two strings they might pull with the administration there. When I'm admitted, I ask them if they kept their promise. They admit that they didn't.

Part II

Regional Qualities; The New Sir

Seventeen to twenty-one

I wanted to go to Dartmouth, where Mike went, but my parents wanted me to go to Swarthmore, if I got in, because it was academically even more distinguished and intense, and because my father met my mother when he lived on the Swarthmore campus and she was at Bryn Mawr, nearby. Bryn Mawr ran in her family—three of her four sisters went there and majored in Classics. My mother will be able to read Greek and Latin into her eighties. The fourth sister went to Radcliffe, and my grandmother considered this to be prodigal. In the thirties, Swarthmore's faculty included a lot of radical professors, and my father, who had dropped out of Cornell after a year or two, felt at home there. He worked for a furniture company in Philadelphia called Charak, to this day in business, still well known. He sold furniture but also designed unique pieces, a few of which I still have, including a long, elegant drop-leaf mahogany dining table that now supports the flat-screen TV in our apartment, above which hangs a Reginald Marsh painting, a gift to my mother from the Ashcan artist, who sometimes did covers for *Fortune*, and who, I believe, had an affair with my mother.

So I go to Swarthmore.

The genuine part of this college's humility proceeds from its Quaker origins. Founded in 1864, the first coed college boarding institution in America, it was a big athletic school for a while, playing football and winning against such behemoths as Ohio State. Then a new President, Frank Aydelotte, who had been impressed by the seminar system at Oxford, instituted the Honors Program for juniors and seniors. Swarthmore's intellectual reputation grew quickly after that and has remained very high since.

The college has a great deal of money, Quaker money, which provides an excellent rationale for students to protest the low wages it pays its maids and cafeteria and grounds employees. These protests seem like training wheels for such impending national movements as Students for a Democratic Society. The college is even more tireless than most institutions in its fund-raising efforts. When I look at the size of its endowment, it sometimes seems that Swarthmore is a bank with students.

The annoying quietude of the Society of Friends is most succinctly expressed in some kind of student-faculty meeting in which a professor responds to an emotional plea for more liberal coed visitation rules, "Everything in moderation." The student mutters, "Yeah, except moderation." (Can you imagine? Men and women are allowed to visit each other in the dorms at Swarthmore only for a few hours on Saturday and Sunday, with the door open. A dean says, "There is no biological reason for college men and women to have sex.")

Balancing that quiet Quaker gentility is Aunt Jane, one of my mother's four sisters, one of the Bryn Mawrers, who lives in Philadelphia and married a Quaker doctor named Maurice McPhedran, converted, and took up *thee*ing and *thou*ing. She once said to a social lingerer: "Thee may stay or thee may leave, but don't ooze!" She sometimes has the sort of sharp proverbial speech I associate with Benjamin Franklin.

A small, self-involved college, Swarthmore tends to flatten outside-world disparities in wealth and prominence. In a radical way, we are all the same. We believe — so wrongly — that we have left our families behind.

I just work so hard. At one point, when I'm a junior, I calculate that I study an average of seven hours every day. The school plays into the obsessiveness in my character and intensifies the competitive legacy of my relationship with my brother. I probably would be doing better, in a number of psychological ways, in a bigger place, one with more air, more students, a stronger relationship to the world at large. Swarthmore broadens my mind vastly. But it narrows me, too.

We live on an island whose population has a kind of mortality rate of twenty-five per cent a year. I look at my dorm room and think, I'll be gone and someone else, maybe with a slide rule and lederhosen, or a clarinet to drive his dorm mates crazy, or with Escher prints everywhere, or with crossed lacrosse sticks hanging up, or with a picture of his girlfriend at Antioch, or with barbells, or with a shrine to Buddha, will be take my place. More than most, I think, I feel the great sadness of undergraduate temporariness, a microcosm of the Great Temporariness, which has frightened me since I was four and comprehended the irremediable deadness of a dead squirrel.

In the cloud chamber of these brief college lives, men grow beards and then shave half of them off. A black woman may wear a turban or a peasant blouse or both. Two friendly subcultures — jocks and frat guys on the one hand and bohemians on the other — look at each other in mild incomprehension across a small social fissure. The girls coalesce into two parallel groups, preppy and bohemian. But enough of us fit into none of these groupings, or any other, to make the place feel pretty free-form. How could I possibly categorize George — quiet, mild-mannered, and undistinctive in every superficial way—who graduates in three years and goes on to the Institute of Advanced Study in Princeton? Shortly before he leaves Swarthmore, he tries to explain to me how he reads equations, the way you are reading this sentence. "A kind of grammar," he says. Or John, who wears a black leather jacket and plays the banjo, rides a motorcycle, and knits during poetry class? (The professor, Mrs. Wright, admits to gender prejudice and makes him stop.) Or Roger, who has an aristocrat's lisp and a shock of dirty-blond hair but sells hero sandwiches in the dorms at night? Or Lucinda, who conducts a psych experiment of getting a few volunteers to wear glasses that turn everything upside-down for three or four days, to find out if upside-down will eventually become right-side-up, and how long that will take.

A Swarthmore senior—the niece of a famous writer—tall and beautiful and shy and brilliant, is going out with a young, tall, blond, brilliant British philosophy professor of renown. With bedazzled freshman eyes, I occasionally see them driving around the campus in his Porsche convertible. But Swarthmore isn't the kind of place that draws celebrities' kids. They go to the Ivy League or to universities on the West Coast—Berkeley, USC, UCLA. But we do have the two Kelly girls—daughters of Gene and, better yet, Walt.

One class behind me at Swarthmore is a guy named Greg, one of the original leaders of SDS. He tells me and some other friends that when he was a little boy, his parents called his penis his "dignity." We're all drunk, at the Tenement, an empty loft across the town line in Morton—Swarthmore is a dry town—which some seniors have rented so that we can go there and drink and dance to Ray Charles records. We all then confess our own parent-inflicted childhood nicknames for private parts and practically fall down laughing. You can stay sitting up, because no, I'm not telling you mine. But how appropriate "dignity" is for the member of a political idealist!

If Swarthmore gives me anything besides a superb liberal-arts education, enhanced academic OCD, and two doomed romances, it gives me a few wonderful lifetime friends and restores my childhood love of folk music, after Nyack's rock-and-roll explosion. (I have a doo-wop radio show on the college's station, which has so little range that you have to rig an antenna to a radiator to receive it at all, and even then you can tune in only within a radius of a few hundred yards of the signal.) Pete Seeger comes to campus and talks, at lunch, about the benefits of outhouses. Who remembers Bonnie Dobson, Canada's pleasant and low-voltage answer to Joan Baez? Blind Reverend Gary Davis sniffs the air as a girl goes by and says, "You lookin' *mighty* good today, child." Ramblin' Jack Elliott, born Elliot Adnopoz, a Brooklyn Jew. The Greenbriar Boys, for whom, for a short time, Bob Dylan is the opening act. The performers include Doc Watson, best flat-picker ever. Ralph Rinzler, a Swarthmore graduate who went on to become the Smithsonian Institution's main folk-music guy.

Phil Ochs comes to the college's annual Folk Festival. Only a few people deeply in the know go to see him, plus a few more happeners-by. The happeners-by get so worked up about Ochs's bright-sounding guitar work and his Klaxon voice and politically defiant lyrics that they start running out of Clothier Hall and grabbing people off the paths and dragging them in to listen. About fifteen minutes after the performance starts, nearly a thousand people fill the place.

We try to latch on to all the roots we can find as we dig our way out of the conventions of the Fifties — Appalachian folk music, the blues, rock and roll, ragas, calypso, gospel. Nerds with slide rules play dulcimers and flail away on banjos and listen to Olatunji, Odetta, and Ochs. Ugly boys from Penn who have learned to play the guitar *really* well come out to Swarthmore and stand and sing on the steps of Parrish Hall, the main administration building, hoping to get laid by one of the free-spirited bohemiennes.

Marijuana for the middle class is just beginning. We disdain it, until we don't—which happens after graduation for most of the kids in my class, '63. But by the time I'm a senior, the Sixties are under way, with their mixture of rebellious music, radical politics, and drugs—serious stuff, but also stuff that socially awkward boys who don't play the guitar can use to get laid.

But my mini-generation, for which there are no letters, no nicknames, marches into Swarthmore studiously, wearing plaid shirts, khakis or jeans (only two brands—Levi's and Lee—and one style each), and sneakers, the ensemble often so ragged that a dress rule is instituted in the dining hall and I resign from the Student Judiciary Committee over this fascistic, anti-populist outrage.

But most of my energy goes to academic work. The professors are excellent. Samuel Hynes teaches the seminar in modern poetry. He flew fighter-bomber missions in the Second World War and by God, if he can like poetry, so can I. He must be one of the best undergraduate humanities professors in America. He starts a discussion of Yeats's "Leda and the Swan"—"A sudden blow: the great wings beating still"—by asking, "Where *are* we here?"

Then there is Hedley Rhys, who teaches the Baroque Painting seminar. A Welshman, precise and mannerly, an expert on Maurice Prendergast, he takes us on a field trip to the Metropolitan Museum in New York, and when we emerge from the Renaissance and begin to look at the Baroque canvases, he asks, "What's different?" and like the child I still am in many ways, I say,

"They're so much bigger!" and he is very pleased. He is also an expert in American accents. He goes around our seminar room — seven students? eight? — at the beginning of the semester and identifies each one accurately. "You're from the Midwest — Ohio, I think," he might say, "but as you're a senior here, you're beginning to pick up some Philadelphia. Be careful." He doesn't get me at first. Then he says, "Say these three words." I remember only one of them: "chocolate." Like the New Yorker I am, I say "chawcolate." He gets New York on this second try, and from that day forward I say "chahcolate."

There is Monroe Beardsley, a small, reedy-voiced philosopher who has written a book called *Aesthetics* which I later come to understand is still the subject's bible. I and thousands of other Swarthmoreans learn about his three measures of artistic achievement, which exist in a wonderful kind of tension with one another: unity, complexity, intensity. About "regional qualities." About how aesthetic value can never be less than zero — there is no bad art, strictly speaking. And we go out into the world with a deepened understanding of the organizing and emotional power of the human mind and imagination, and a greater capacity to see, hear, read, and comprehend. And be caught up and moved.

Then there is Helen North, who teaches a course called Classical Mythology in Art and Literature, a panoptic survey of the variations in and implications of the use of Greek divinities in Homer, Ovid, Dante, and many others — the reading list is a backbreaker — and in visual representations through the ages. She is a brilliant lecturer who seems to assume that we are all conversant with her references — and so we strive to be.

I don't know it at the time, but these humanities courses and seminars — demanding, deep, wide in their scope — constitute not only an intellectual but an emotional preparation for the work

I will later do and the losses I will suffer. If you are lucky enough to be educated *well* in an ivory tower, it will help to prepare you to descend from that tower and deal with un-ivoried reality. When your heart is broken, Yeats will give the heartbreak a grand context. When there's a death in the family, Hans Bol's painting of a plowman with Icarus falling in the very distant distance may help to comfort you about the necessity of life to go on. When your work becomes tedious, Sisyphus will trudge along by your side. When you're praised, you will remember, prophylactically, Marc Antony's praise of Brutus. If you have children, Joe Gargery will coach you in good cheer. When you blame yourself mightily for a sin, the logical positivists may offer some small comfort with compelling arguments against free will. When you see your five-year-old daughter's marvelous painting entitled "Francis Dines with Claire," with the couple sitting at opposite ends of a long table and a dog eating scraps below, your Intro to Psych course and reading of Freud will make you wonder about the separation, and Hedley Rhys will re-materialize to point out the childlike directness and distortions of some of Picasso's late work.

Everything in your life is enriched, everything has a more universal human context. And just when you are feeling pleased with your own shaky semi-erudition, Yeats will reappear to remind you that

> *On their own feet they came, or on shipboard,*
> *Camel-back, horse-back, ass-back, mule-back,*
> *Old civilisations put to the sword.*
> *Then they and their wisdom went to rack:*
> *No handiwork of Callimachus,*
> *Who handled marble as if it were bronze,*
> *Made draperies that seemed to rise*

When sea-wind swept the corner, stands;
His long lamp-chimney shaped like the stem
Of a slender palm, stood but a day;
All things fall and are built again. . . .

And then, antidotally to this message of transience, you may read aloud to yourself the pure, sharp music of the line "Camel-back, horse-back, ass-back, mule-back." What daring is *that*, from a poet who started out writing about Celtic faeries!

Nineteen

At the end of my sophomore year at Swarthmore, I am about to enter the Honors Program, in which juniors and seniors have only two three-hour seminars a week, one in their major and one in one or the other of their minors. (Mine are, respectively, English Literature, and Art History and Philosophy. Not exactly vocational training.) I explain to Mr. Becker, the head of the English Department, that my soccer practices and games the following fall may occasionally conflict with afternoon seminars. He says, "We can't schedule morning meetings for one person, Mr. Menaker." He adds, "Especially when the conflict involved could hardly have less to do with academic endeavors."

The one time soccer does conflict with an Honors seminar — Problems in Modern Philosophy, which is all about positivism (A. J. Ayer and his "sense data," Strawson, Wittgenstein, Ryle, Quine) — Professor Jerome Shaffer takes the whole class down to the soccer field on a beautiful fall day to watch the team play.

Professor Shaffer goes on to be the Chairman of the Philosophy Department at the University of Connecticut and then retires in order to learn and practice psychotherapy.

Twenty

Richard Nixon's Presidential-campaign motorcade makes its way through the town of Swarthmore. He's going to stop and give a short speech from a platform in the middle of town. He walks through the crowd, shaking hands, and a friend of mine, David Gelber, editor of the college newspaper, later to become a producer for *60 Minutes*, finds himself in Nixon's path. He dislikes Nixon. When Nixon sticks out his hand for Gelber to shake, he does so, involuntarily, but at the last second tries to express his distaste by muttering, sarcastically, "How's Checkers?" (Nixon's dog.) Nixon climbs up on the platform, thanks a few people for setting up the event, and says, "I especially want to thank that very nice young man in the crowd who was kind enough to ask after our dog, Checkers. I'm happy to say that Checkers is just fine."

Back at school, I have a girl in my dorm room overnight. She gets her period and there is blood on the sheets. I forget that this is the day when the sheets get changed, and I certainly have no idea that the house mother of our dorm will be accompanying the maid on her rounds that particular sheet-changing day. The house mother reports me to the Dean of Men. I am scared shitless. He calls me into his office, but I say I can't see him until the next day—after an exam. I go out to the cinder track around the football field wearing shorts and sink to the ground a few times, lacerating my knees nicely. I wear the shorts when I go to see the Dean the next morning. I'm sure he knows what's up, but he just lets it go. Back at the dorm, I find that the maid has stripped the bed and washed the sheets. "I know how boys and girls is," she whispers to me.

It's the spring of my senior year and I am taking Honors exams— eight three-hour written exams and eight oral exams, all administered by professors from other colleges. I have studied for these tests for three months in the spring, according to a lunatic-obsessive schedule I made for myself. The exams seem to be going well for me. During my oral exam in Baroque Painting, a stout, tweed-jacketed, thick-and-glossy-bearded professor from the University of Pennsylvania takes a copy of Rembrandt's late painting *The Descent from the Cross* from his small pile of such reproductions. He asks me to talk about it. I say what I know, including the comment from a recent article in a scholarly journal about the artist's use of "irrational" light sources in his late work.

"You read that piece?" the examiner says, smiling. "I'm impressed." Then he goes on. "But the thesis about light sources is wrong. Look." We look at the reproduction together, and he shows me that the lighting of the scene, though extremely dramatic, isn't, strictly speaking, irrational. He takes other late Rembrandt paintings from his little stack, and we discuss their brooding, luminous use of light and the possibility that the artist's failing vision may have affected this aspect of his painting. I mention that I've read that El Greco may have had astigmatism, which could account for the elongation of figures in his late paintings. The examiner says, "Also wrong, in my opinion, but arguable. Just because a professor or a scholarly journal says something doesn't make it right." He smiles a merry and mischievous smile. "Now," he says, "here's another Rembrandt, this one with some of the background painted by his apprentices."

"No," I say.

"Why not?"

Rembrandt didn't use apprentices—like Rubens did.

When the Honors-exams results are posted in the spring of my senior year, Mr. Hynes invites me and my friend Leo Braudy to have drinks and dinner with him and his wife. Leo gets Highest Honors, I get High Honors, and by God I will take it. When we arrive at his house, Mr. Hynes comes out and greets us. He puts his arms around our shoulders and says, "My boys!" I get so drunk that evening that I pass out on the couch in Mr. Hynes's study. The next morning, I get up with the worst hangover ever, and Mr. Hynes offers me a glass of orange juice. "This will cut the phlegm," he says.

Twenty-one to twenty-three

I go to graduate school in English at Johns Hopkins on a teaching fellowship for two years and get a Master's degree. The first year, I rent a room on the top floor of a tidy marble-step row house near the Hopkins Homewood campus in Baltimore. A country-club bandleader named Billy owns the house and lives there with his mother and his girlfriend. He has an organ on which he practices and rearranges in the least imaginative way possible the least interesting big-band tunes and pop-song adaptations imaginable. He seems addicted to the Serendipity Singers' "Don't Let the Rain Come Down," a pabulum crime committed against the words of the nursery rhyme that starts "There was a crooked man." Billy attacks this song organistically again and again, late into the night, the "melody" to the refrain—"Ah ah, oh no, don't let the rain come down"—repeated with minuscule changes to rhythm and phrasing and "improvisation." It is maddening. He keeps practicing this song even through the trauma of President Kennedy's assassination. His girlfriend, a blowzy woman with the daffy-lipstick look, weeps uncontrollably over this event. Billy takes a little time off from "Don't Let the Rain Come Down" to invite me to watch the funeral on his television. His girlfriend sobs on the couch. "You know, Audrey knew the Kennedys," Billy says to me.

The American Literature guy at Hopkins, Professor Charles Anderson, requires us to buy his anthologies. J. Hillis Miller, a nice man who teaches Victorian fiction and is apparently a genius of literary theory, talks about Derrida's writing and other abstruse critical doctrines of the moment. I haven't got the faintest idea what he's talking about. I am deemed a good Freshman Composition teacher because on the day I'm "observed," I answer a student's question with "It's a noun clause." There are a couple of serene young Jesuit scholars in the graduate program who appear to know everything. An inch and a half of snow falls and hysterical Baltimore drivers abandon their cars in the middle of main thoroughfares. At least beer is cheap. I see women in bars giving their babies bottles with a little beer in them, as if out of a cautionary nineteenth-century temperance pamphlet. The second place I live, during the second year, features a Havishamian landlady the door to whose ground-floor apartment opens a crack whenever one of her boarders comes or goes.

It isn't for me. The *Lucky Jim*–ish Best Toady contest for thesis advisers, the danger of saddling up on a hobbyhorse like "subject-object relations" and riding it for the rest of my life, the booing of the Yankees when they play at Memorial Stadium — not for me. But I do read and study an enormous amount at Hopkins, especially about one of the literary-theory fashions of the time, point of view, which will serve me well in my professional life. And once again, I have some very good teachers, and German semi-learned, and a degree and two years' teaching experience that will guarantee me a job in a private school and another Vietnam War draft deferment.

Earl Wasserman alone is worth the price of admission, pursuing the Romantics like an eager tailor and jamming them into a one-size-fits-all theory with remarkable success.

Twenty-two

It's summertime and I'm home from graduate school. Pete Seeger gives a concert in Nyack, at the Tappan Zee Playhouse. My uncle Enge is visiting us, and he and I decide to go to the performance. Afterward we go backstage to say hello to Seeger—Enge says he knows him—but he doesn't recognize my uncle at all. Enge is humiliated and insists that they have met, that they called square dances together at the Henry Street Settlement, on the Lower East Side of Manhattan. This incident will have a surprising epilogue thirty-five years later.

Another summer weekend, Mike comes home to Nyack. My girlfriend is there, too. Mike and "Precious"—my mother gave her that nickname when she heard her use the word, with her Southern accent and all—want to go to Jones Beach, on Long Island. It's a long drive and I don't feel like going. I tell the two of them to go ahead.

They go, and they come back. Later, my girlfriend says to me, "Why did you let me go with him alone?"

"Why not?" I say. "I didn't want to go and the two of you did."

"Don't you know anything? Didn't it occur to you that I might begin to fall in love with him if we spent that kind of time together?"

Twenty-three

Earl Wasserman, at Johns Hopkins, reads a paper on Bernard Malamud's *The Natural,* explicating its (pretty obvious) allegorical details. After the reading is over, one of my fellow–graduate students presents him with a baseball signed by various Baltimore Orioles. Embarrassingly close to an apple for the teacher, given by a grown man (a hefty grown man at that, and a Rhodes Scholar).

I go to Memorial Stadium, near the Homewood campus, when the Yankees play the Orioles there. In the bleachers, I keep my Yankee fandom to myself. Whitey Ford, the Yankee ace, is pitching one day, and the Orioles knock him out of the game in the third or fourth inning. A delighted guy sitting next to me takes a white handkerchief out of his pocket and waves it mockingly. "Goodbye, Mr. Edward Whitey Ford," he calls out as Ford walks off the mound. "Goodbye, Mr. Edward Whitey Ford," he shouts again, and claps me on the back.

These two years spent in Baltimore make me realize that, one way or another, I am eventually going to end up back in New York.

The "new journalist" Tom Wolfe publishes a piece in *New York* magazine called "Tiny Mummies," a funny, caricatured picture of *The New Yorker* in all its crazy cultishness, and a close portrait of its editor, William Shawn. In the piece, Wolfe conveys the hermetic, self-involved, highly ritualized life of the magazine's staff in telling detail. And he distills his whole experience there when he describes what happened when he asked Shawn, in Shawn's office, if he could smoke. Shawn was apparently nonplused by the request and responded with a kind of frantic over-obligingness. He scrambled around looking for an ashtray, and when he couldn't find one, he offered Wolfe an empty soda bottle. Anyone who has smoked and tried to tap his ashes into a soda bottle knows that it doesn't work well, so Wolfe found himself trying with manual subtlety to get the ashes from his cigarette into this undersized aperture and watching as a kind of tutu of errant ashes formed around the base of the bottle—which he and Shawn pretended not to notice.

I happen to read this piece, and I think, "It sounds like graduate school!" I know my mother and father look forward to reading

The New Yorker every week. My mother subscribed to the magazine from its very start, in 1925. I know all the famous pieces that have been published there. There's a kind of call-and-response I've noticed among my elders: When adults say *"The New Yorker,"* other adults say "Hiroshima" or "Silent Spring" or "The Fire Next Time." But still, in the piece by Wolfe, it's a madhouse of genteel repression, a mild Maoism. Who would want to work there? Me.

I've just gotten my Master's degree in English from Hopkins and have decided not to go back to graduate school. Instead, I'll teach English at the George School, in Bucks County, Pennsylvania, come September. But for the summer I'm living in Nyack and working nearby as a toll taker on the New York State Thruway, at the Spring Valley toll barrier. I with my Master's and its focus on Romantic Poetry. The regular toll takers are mostly retired cops, on half-pay pensions for life and supplementing that income. The contempt they have for the public, especially the Jews who drive up by the vanful from the Bronx and Brooklyn every Friday before sunset to go to their resorts and bungalows in the Catskills, is impressive. "Here come the Bronx Indians!" they yell to each other starting around 4 p.m. "Vitch vay to deh mountings?" they ask each other. "Same vay last veek," they answer. "No, no— *kveek*-vay, *kveek*-vay!" (There is some kind of shortcut off the Thruway farther north.) "Kveek-vay also same vay last veek."

The work is so boring, especially when I'm on the side that just gives out the tickets rather than receiving tolls and making change, that I start handing the tickets out by reaching around behind my back. Most of the "patrons" seem to enjoy this tiny variation. Some express annoyance. Men in a hurry.

Speaking of which, it is my sexist observation/conclusion that men have their tolls ready and women do not. Many females root around in their purses, which are often lying on the passenger seat beside them. One of the other toll takers says that they are rummaging around in there looking for the male private parts they don't have. He doesn't put it exactly that way.

Some patrons don't bother with tolls at all: Every now and then over the summer, gypsies arrive at the barrier and make up complicated stories about having lost their toll coupons or whatever. It's not worth pulling over a caravan of four or five trailers and old-fashioned wagons, so they are generally allowed to go on through.

One toll taker's nickname is Vampira. Nobody knows anything about her. She always takes the midnight-to-8 a.m. shift, is skeletally thin, chalk pale, and hardly ever says a word to anyone.

As I've said, it will occur to me when I'm seventy, as I sit waiting for yet more medical tests — a PET scan and a simulation for some high-tech radiation treatments — that inhaling all that car exhaust may not have caused me to get lung cancer but it wasn't exactly preventive, either. Especially as emissions standards were a thing of the distant future. On a hot, still July day at the Spring Valley toll plaza, the air felt, smelled, and tasted like vaporized, rancid butter infused with gasoline fumes.

Sometimes the endless procession of automobiles strikes me as a march of monsters along a wide swath of flat, man-made insult to nature. Cars begin to take on a surreal implausibility — tons of metal often, usually, carrying a single human being oblivious of the peculiarity of the dreadful mechanical complexities his species' overgrown frontal lobe has wrought. The traffic parade also reminds me of my time as a waiter at the Guest Camp, with the guests sitting and eating all at the same time — seventy, eighty, a hundred of them at long tables of ten, working their jaws, spooning up soup, forking London broil. I would sit on the porch rail and watch, and the scene would turn into a Boschian nightmare. To this day, I sometimes divide people psychologically into those who have waited on tables and those who haven't.

Twenty-three to twenty-six

The kids—boys and girls—who go to the George School, in Bucks County, sometimes seem radically bereft to me. No matter how you try to dress it up in the garments of a good Quaker education, an idyllic campus, good athletic facilities, and so on, these kids have been sent away to school. I swear you can see sadness in their faces when they don't know you're looking. And you know how lucky you were to have stayed home—even a home with Problems—in a home worth staying home in.

But that may just be me, projecting like a modern-day Imax my own separation anxiety of such long duration. I will never be close to completely rid of it. And many if not most of the kids are no doubt better off away from home. Every now and then I get a small hint of real trouble in their families.

Teaching composition to undergraduates at Hopkins was one thing—basically technical, well suited to my nearly inborn deep grammatical structure, no in-loco-parentis expectations—and teaching fourteen-year-olds is another. I don't know what I'm doing. I'm boring. As I write this, I can't remember what books we read, what kinds of papers I assigned, or very much about the individual students, although a few non-academic moments have stayed with me.

One: An Ethiopian exchange student, brand new to this school and this country, reports for outdoor phys ed in a ribbed white undershirt and white Jockey briefs.

Another: A wily kid offers to exchange a pretty good tape

recorder for the prized '52 Series Fender Telecaster I got for my sixteenth birthday. I don't realize the inequity of this swap, but it doesn't matter, because I wasn't ever going to play the electric guitar anyway. It was a momentary passion that my indulgent parents indulged. The kid apologizes to me later, and I tell him to forget about it.

Another: A young teacher friend of mine gets a senior girl in trouble and marries her.

Another: A smart and lovely senior girl gets what I call now a "structural crush" on me and looks me up in New York after she graduates and turns eighteen.

Another: I launch a literary magazine, and we announce it at a school-wide assembly by means of a funny and iconoclastic skit I write, involving students standing up in the audience and proclaiming their authorial genius, or denouncing the whole project as propaganda, or reading awful poetry.

Another: I take one of the poems I've been writing and submitting in vain to *The New Yorker* and copy it and give it, without a byline, to one of my classes to criticize and analyze—this occurs when the head of the English Department happens to be attending the class. Observation. The students pick it apart, and I join in the general disparagement, pointing out affectations and lame tropes and sentimentality. When I tell them, at the end of the class, that I wrote it, they—and my boss—are delighted.

But I find the sequestered and bucolic life of a boarding-school teacher stifling. I eat all my meals with students, I am the resident in a small dorm, and I can't see the girl I'm going out with as much as I'd like; she's taking acting classes in Manhattan. After four years at Swarthmore and two at Hopkins, I keenly miss New York and Nyack. So I apply for and get a job teaching at the Collegiate School, on the Upper West Side.

∙ ∙ ∙

Collegiate, the oldest private school in America, differs as much from the George School as public school in Nyack did from the Little Red School House. And there are no girls. The students are more worldly and streetwise. They go home at night after carousing through the bars with fake IDs. Many are the sons of rich people and professors and attorneys. There is a Bronfman there, an Ausubel, a Dupee, a Kristol, a Bartos. A contingent of black and Hispanic kids descend from Manhattan's upper, poorer reaches and attend Collegiate on scholarship, under a program called ABC—A Better Chance. They're usually among the best athletes in the school, and they sometimes manage to form friendships with the privileged boys, but more often don't. The Castilian-speaking Spanish teacher flunks a Puerto Rican kid in Spanish I.

The students have to wear jackets and ties. The ties grow very wide and floral. This is 1966, 1967, 1968, after all. The pupils (the parts of the eye, I mean) are often similarly wide. When I first arrive, I laugh when the students in my classes call me "Sir"—as they are required to do. After a while I come to like it. On my third day, I hear a usage of the word that I like even more and that contains an inadvertent compliment, about my work and about my looks. A kid says to me in passing, in the hall, "Are you in that new Sir's class? He teaches English. I hear he's going to be pretty good." I say, "I am in one of the new Sir's classes. I'm in all of them, because I'm the new Sir. So thank you." The kid says, "Wow! You look too young to be a Sir, Sir."

The smarter students feel free to argue with teachers about anything. In a doctrinaire way—I should know better but am feeling my authority more confidently at this point—I talk about Macduff's sterling character in *Macbeth*, and one of the boys is able to fluster me by citing a far more negative interpretation of his motives from a respected critic. My second year at the school, I teach an Advanced Placement course in American Literature and assign readings from the Puritans, especially Jonathan Edwards, to Hawthorne to Melville to Poe to James to Hemingway, with some stops in between. The students complain about the workload and the tediousness of the Puritan material, and the Headmaster, Carl Andrews, talks to me about it, and I feel a little abashed, as if I have somehow been showing off with this ambitious curriculum. But I keep on with it, too embarrassed to stop. Not knowing exactly how to stop. But also how much I myself have learned out of doggedness.

The students in the class are seniors. The next year, when coming back to Collegiate to visit, three or four of them, mostly the whiniest, tell me how helpful the course was in their college English classes — which is not only a compliment but a reaffirmation of the delayed gratifications of persistence.

In that senior class, on Parents' Day, I criticize the Introduction to James's *Daisy Miller* as being more biographical than literarily enlightening. One of the visiting fathers comes up to me when the class is over and says how much he enjoyed the class. I ask him which his son is. "Tony," he says. That would be Tony Dupee. Which means that the man thanking me is F. W. Dupee, one of the leading American Literature scholars in the world. So the compliment grows even more rewarding. Until I remember that it was Professor Dupee who wrote that Introduction. My mistake.

"Don't worry," he says as I redden. "It was a really good class and your criticism made sense. Although I can't help defending myself — that's the trouble with academics. I *meant* the Introduction to be biographical, for those who were reading the book — and maybe James — for the first time."

My brother Mike has graduated from law school at the University of Virginia. Law school has made him more studious and somber. He gets serious about the girlfriend who soon ends up his wife and never tells intimate stories about her. Well, maybe a little, at the start. He begins to criticize my immaturities, which are many, in a more sober way. When he's hired by a fancy law firm in New York—Davis, Polk—courtesy of a UVA Law professor who took a liking to him and overlooked his just-shy-of-stellar grades, he finds the work overwhelmingly difficult and tells me glumly that he doesn't think he will ever be made a partner there. He is starting to carry the weight of adulthood, in other words, and in doing so once again shows me the way. I don't like the way and don't follow it—I don't want to have any part of this weightiness. I'm teaching at Collegiate and still want my summers off, my work hours limited, my personal life "free." And I want Mike to be my brother as he has always been, when we were kids and teenagers and undergraduates. I want time to stop for us. I'm jealous of his relationship with his wife. I think I'm losing him, and in a way I am. This is Mike's hardest fraternal task—putting a stop to my childhood. He succeeds, ultimately, but in a way so devastating to me and my family that I think the worst villain would not have willed it to happen.

It's Thanksgiving of 1967, and we're playing touch football before dinner with some Grace cousins from Boston on the front lawn of the house in Nyack. It's a pure fall day, with the Hudson all blue and white, the tree branches vascular-looking in their bareness, and the air as clean and clear as alcohol. Mike's wife and my girlfriend are standing on the sidelines. Before the game starts, I try to tease him about something, and when he doesn't respond, I grab him around the waist and try to wrestle him to the ground. He shakes me off and says, "Why don't you grow up?" I'm embarrassed and angry.

The game begins, with me and Mike against the Graces. Because he has bad knees and has already had surgery on one of them, Mike plays the more static lineman position and I play backfield. Still consciously smarting from his scolding, I finally say, "I'm tired. You play backfield for once." My mistake. Mike says, "You know I can't." I say, "Your precious knees will be fine." He says OK. On the very first play, he jumps to try to knock down a pass and comes down with one of his legs all twisted up. It buckles beneath him and he tears a knee ligament. He is furious, and his wife glares at me. I'm covered with remorse and apologize to them. Mike hobbles through the rest of the holiday and has surgery in the first week of December.

On the day after the surgery, in Brooklyn, Carl Andrews walks into my classroom at Collegiate and tells me to call my parents at the hospital in Brooklyn where Mike was operated on. I go out of the classroom and dial, then stand there, next to the wall phone, listening to my mother try, without crying, to tell me that something has gone wrong. And that same dreadful feeling of cold and abandonment which descended on me in Grand Central Terminal fifteen years earlier descends on me again. In this terror, I'm surprised to feel my knees go weak—I didn't know it ever really happened, outside of metaphor.

My brother lies in a semi-private hospital room in Brooklyn. In view of his critical condition, the room's other patient and the doctors agree that Mike should have the room to himself. The roommate is moved out. Mike has septicemia—a vicious, systemic blood infection that he must have contracted during the surgery, which was a routine procedure to repair the ligament injury he sustained when we were playing football.

I have a cold and I ask the resident if it's a bad idea to go into Mike's room and talk to him. The resident says it's probably OK, but if I want to be on the safe side, it might be best just to stand in the doorway. That's what I want to hear, because the truth is that I don't want to get near my brother. I am terrified of his perilous condition—he's conscious but very, very sick—and I don't know how I would act or what I would say if I got close to him.

My mother and father and girlfriend and sister-in-law and I sit in a typically inhospitable hospital waiting room. My brother had come back to consciousness after having been unresponsive for some time. But the doctors say that he is still in great danger—they say it in such a way as to make me sure that my brother is going to die. My mother encourages me to go to Mike's room and talk to him. I get up and go down the hall and stand in the doorway.

"I almost bought the farm," Mike says.

"I know," I say. "You had us all really scared, even though I knew you were probably faking."

My brother smiles his dazzling smile. He's not even thirty and looks even younger now, and in such danger. He is lying on his back, his head on a thin pillow, so he is looking at me with lowered eyes, half-lidded, as if he were in a waking dream, or watching out for an attack from below. His voice is dreamy, too. "And how are you, my young scholar?"

"I have a cold or I'd go over there and straighten you out," I say.

"And how is Precious?" he asks.

"She's fine—she's here too."

"How can someone so good-looking stand to be seen with you?"

I am out of wisecracks.

"I almost bought the farm," he says.

"Two farms," I say.

"What?"

"Never mind. You know you're going to be fine, right?"

"I don't think so. I really feel bad all of a sudden."

"Well, I'll go back and get the doctor or a nurse. Hang in there."

"OK—I'll see you later," he says.

I leave the room and tell a nurse passing by that my brother says he's feeling pretty bad. She goes into his room and I go back to the waiting room.

It turns out that his coming-to is only temporary. He goes into a coma, and all his vital organs begin to slowly shut down as the infection, resistant to the strongest available antibiotics, spreads. The hospital allows us all to stay in small, functional apartments that are generally used for interns and nurses. I call Collegiate and say that I won't be able to return to teaching for a while. In the daytime, we sit in that waiting room with its cheese-rind hues. My sister-in-law sits on a couch, closing and opening a fist, saying that as long as she does so, Mike's heart will keep beating.

It doesn't.

Mike's friends from Dartmouth come to Nyack to pay their respects. Dave Hiley, Alex Summer, the Good McGinnis, the Bad McGinnis, Arnie Sigler, Otter, Roger Zissu. Seeing these young men—still boys, in some ways—is unbearable. They cast their eyes down, don't know how to act, what to say. How could they? They have had no occasion to learn comportment for such a disaster. As is only proper. And they can't help it, but they fairly *glow* with energy and youth. Dave Hiley approaches me in the back yard and I put my hand on his shoulder—to keep him away, to draw him close, to keep myself from falling to the ground in grief.

The funeral, conducted by my sister-in-law's uncle, the Reverend Francis Sayre, Dean of the Washington National Cathedral, takes place in an Episcopal church in Manhattan, Mike's Jewish nipples notwithstanding. Everyone there—and there are hundreds and hundreds—looks sick and white, as if some terrible epidemic has struck them.

Two years after my brother's death, researchers develop an antibiotic that effectively combats hospital-acquired staphylococcus septicemia.

Twenty-six to fifty or so

When I tell people about this event in detail — as I do seldom and only when the conversation makes doing so unavoidable — they tend to wince as I describe how Mike was injured. As if they themselves have been hurt and as if they sense how deeply I have wounded myself. Because look — I know it's true that I didn't take a vial of staph bacteria and pour it into the incision during surgery, and I know that the accident's outcome was violently random and arbitrary, and I know that we all tend to take responsibility for things we aren't responsible for. But on the other hand, try telling me that there's no chance that my brother would be alive today if I hadn't done what I did. Try not to grimace when you think of the causal chain that led to my brother's organs shutting down one after another way out in Brooklyn, where there weren't even any tall buildings to add some grandeur to his death.

That challenge isn't as bitter as it sounds. I really *was* still just a kid then, I realize. Twenty-six. And after decades of hard psychological work and simply getting on with things, I've forgiven myself, and I understand that what all of us have done is surely what we were going to do. The past is the definition of inevitability. And as the years have gone by and the broken emotional bones have knitted, I've come to understand and appreciate not only what I lost in this catastrophe but what I found. I'm good at consoling others, for one thing. And this is not a small thing, especially recently, as the casualties of ordinary life have begun to mount among family and friends. Petty reversals, my own or others', remain more or less where they should among my concerns—way down on the ladder. I do whatever I can to shape my future but when it becomes the past, I can leave it alone back there pretty well. Nothing to be done except learn from it. I think I respond even more deeply to art, music, and literature because of the lesson in life's fragility I unwillingly learned from my brother's death. And as my parents' suddenly only child, I assumed and carried out a kind of lonely responsibility toward them, especially as they got older.

And there's this: About ten years after Mike dies, it begins to dawn on me that his death will ultimately leave me in better financial shape than I would have been if he had lived—my parents' modest estate undivided, Enge's house and land in the country similarly wholly mine. This comes as an almost overnight surprise to me, I'm ashamed to be proud to say—it has never once entered my mind before then—and it makes me feel good and awful at the same time. Good because the inheritance situation has at least had the decency to wait a decade to occur to me. Bad because it means I'd won the battle between us. Somewhere in my hideous id, I killed him. I vanquished him from the field, and the spoils are all mine. And the only thing worse on a primal human level than Oedipal defeat is Oedipal victory. This one, in conjunction with early-childhood illnesses and askew family geometry, has been making intimacy difficult for me for decades.

But then there's this: literally this. It allows me to write. It compels me to write. For five or six months I was so paralyzed by sorrow and dismay that it was all I could do simply to function. To go back to Collegiate and teach. To try to figure out how to talk to my parents. To brush off kind inquiries from colleagues and students, for fear that if I gave in to what pressed down on me so hard, I would never get up. And then out of desperation I wrote a story based on what had happened. And then came more writing—because much as I dislike the actual work of writing, it settles me, makes me feel as though I am actually managing myself, as nothing else does. I suppose this goes in the plus column too.

But finally there's this: Would I give back every sentence, every lesson learned, every bit of wisdom, every gram of sympathy for others, every sensitivity, every penny, every square inch of real estate, to have Mike walking three years ahead of me? Instead of adding year after unnatural year to my seniority over him? Instead of coming around the bend of the year and into the fall with the usual schoolboy's summer's-end sadness so uniquely sharpened? Instead of living in the shadow of an alternative unlived life? You tell me.

Twenty-seven

Tom McDade, Mike's and my godfather and the former FBI man who investigated my father and someone who lost *his* brother when they were both young, visits us in Nyack after Mike's death and, unprompted, says to me, "I know you think you'll never get over this, but you will—I promise." And, well, eventually I will. Over it but, obviously, not through with it.

I've been teaching English at the Collegiate School for two years. Now that I'm over twenty-six, over draft age, I decide to leave teaching.

The Headmaster, Carl Andrews, is an excellent man—a little short, a little heavy, a heavy smoker, very smart and decent, always scooting around from one responsibility to another, a great basketball fan, and extremely proud of and fatherly toward the school's students, with their startling ties and dope-widened eyes.

Carl tells me that when Jacqueline Kennedy was considering Collegiate for her young son, John, he had shown the two of them around the school and its new building. Mrs. Kennedy kept saying things like, "If John is accepted, would there be an orientation for new boys in the fall?" and "If John is accepted, I assume we'd need to provide you with records from his previous school." Carl finally stopped in the middle of a hallway, drew Mrs. Kennedy aside, and said, quietly, "Mrs. Kennedy, I think it's safe for me to say that John is accepted at Collegiate."

I laughed, but for a few minutes this story struck me as being a poor reflection on the Headmaster's integrity. I could hear Enge and my father saying, "You see?" I did see. But I was also continuing to learn that, as in the English Department at Hopkins, influence and connection are always part of the way of the world. And that Carl has been treating me like an adult by confessing his own—and understandable—susceptibility to influence, not so much for the sake of this fortunate unfortunate child as for the sake of the school.

"I'm sorry, but I'm not coming back next fall," I tell Carl in the late spring of 1968.

He gets angry. "This is a real problem, Dan," he says. "This means we have to find a replacement in an impossibly short time."

My mistake. I feel awful. I haven't given a single thought to the predicament I am putting the school into. "I'm really sorry," I say again. "I guess I didn't realize—"

"You should have. This is just typical of the selfishness of some young people today. It really speaks poorly of you."

Desperate to regain some sort of footing, I remember an incident from the previous fall. "Well, you're not the only disappointed one here," I say.

"What do you mean?"

"Remember you told me that I would be named head of the English Department next fall?"

"What?"

"You said with Henry Adams leaving, I'd be head of the department. And then a couple of weeks ago you appointed Pete."

Carl pauses, looks stymied. "You're absolutely right," he says. "I went back on my word. I guess I have no right to be criticizing you this way."

Well, what do you know! He made a mistake and admitted it—which reminded me of his candor about young John Kennedy's acceptance to Collegiate. He was showing me exactly the kind of adulthood that, with my thoughtless announcement of departure, I was still a considerable way from achieving.

Part III

The Drudge;
Alex Trebek's Constitution

Twenty-seven

It's May of 1968. Without a new job in the offing, despondent, girlfriend with good sense gone back to the South. Family devastated. My widowed sister-in-law comes to visit in Nyack, and I hear her and my mother practically barking, they are weeping so violently upstairs. My father's early signs of dementia become more pronounced — mercifully, maybe.

What will become of me? Before I have to decide — I couldn't decide anyway — my uncle Enge's young lover, Tom Waddell, makes the United States Olympic Team in the decathlon. Tom had been a counselor at my uncle Pete's boys' camp during the summers he was in college, at Springfield, and that's how he and Enge met. The Olympics will take place in Mexico City, and so with four or five others, family and friends, I go to watch him compete. I see Tommie Smith and John Carlos raise their fists in the Black Power salute. I watch Bob Beamon shatter the world long-jump record by a foot and a half. The crowd *groans* with astonishment when he does it.

Tom swipes a U.S. Olympic Team sweatshirt and sweatpants for me. The outfit allows me to go with him into the locker rooms and staging areas for the events being held at the Olympic Stadium in Mexico City. The young men there are often half dressed or naked. They look like Phidian sculptures brought to life and forward to the twentieth century. As with the caliber of their performance in the events they compete in, the physical appearance of these guys puts to eternal rest my fantasies of ever having been or being a good athlete. Except for one sport—tennis—which to this day I believe I could have excelled in, if only I had started lessons early enough, instead of trying to pick the game up in my late twenties. I have the slightly bowed, slightly short legs of many a tennis pro, very quick reflexes, and nothing else but such fantasies.

Tom finishes sixth in the decathlon. Do you have any idea how good and complete an athlete you have to be to do that? As I'm watching him achieve personal bests in many of the ten events, I remember when my brother—my late brother—and a few friends and cousins played not only basketball but touch football the day before his wedding, in Princeton, at my sister-in-law's family's house. I threw the ball as a "kickoff," and Tom caught it and ran it back like a phantom. He seemed to disappear when you tried to tag him and scored a touchdown. Without a word, we all realized that there was no point in continuing.

Mike had insisted on playing on the line in that game, worried about his knee.

I get back from the Olympics, hang around doing nothing, answer an ad in the *Times* for an editorial assistant at Prentice Hall. Somehow that company, largely a producer of textbooks, had come to publish the bestseller *Up the Down Staircase,* and the executives there decided that they could expand into trade-book publishing, competing against Simon & Schuster and Viking and Random House and all the rest. It couldn't, but when I'm interviewed for the job, they think they're going to go great guns.

I get the job and have to reverse-commute, from the Upper West Side, where I've been sharing an apartment with a friend from Swarthmore while teaching at Collegiate, to Englewood, New Jersey, every day in a car pool. I sit in a cubicle with less idea of what I'm doing there than I had when J. Hillis Miller talked about Derrida and de Man in graduate school. The guy I'm working for takes me into the city at around noon from time to time to have a publishing lunch. He talks to agents and writers, but I have no idea what kind of progress is being made, what kind of business is being done. It seems absurd to travel for an hour to get to lunch, have lunch for an hour and a half, and drive an hour back from lunch, but that's Englewood for you. Publishing, I learn later, is a little like the garment industry: You have to be geographically well placed, in New York, for schmoozing convenience.

Sometimes I'm given a book proposal to read and report on. I write the report. Nothing happens.

One of my first cousins is Janet Bingham. She is the daughter of Aunt Jane McPhedran, the one who asked in Quakerese that departing dinner guests not "ooze." Janet's husband, Robert Bingham, is an editor at *The New Yorker*. He calls me one day, six months into my Prentice Hall cryptojob, and asks if I'd like to try for a Fact Checker position at the magazine. Someone has left and he is close enough to my family to remember that I'm emotionally and occupationally adrift. My mother, an Original Subscriber, is in her quiet way clearly pleased about this possibility.

I try. I get the job. Even though I have this family connection to the place, I like to believe that I get it on my own merits, even if they are principally sartorial: After my interview, as I walk out of the office, I see that the man who interviewed me — Leo Hofeller, the executive editor — has written on top of my résumé "*Well-groomed!*" His desk was covered with yellow-highlighted racing forms. He was wearing a gray pin-striped suit and wing-tip cordovans. His gray hair was combed back; it looked wing-tipped, too.

Before that interview, I sat waiting in the nineteenth-floor lobby, near a huge, round, and mystifying brazier-like table. A rodential miniature poodle with off-white fur wandered out of an office and into the waiting area. A tall, bald, distinguished-looking man wearing glasses came down the stairs behind me from the twentieth floor, saw the dog, approached it, got very close, and loomed forward over it. This sent the dog into a paroxysm of angry barking. The man turned around, looked at me, put his fingers to his lips, and quickly made his way down the hall. A few seconds later, a little woman with curly hair ducked out of the same office nearby, agitated, and said, "Goldie, Goldie—what's wrong?" She looked at me. "What happened?" she said. I shrugged my shoulders.

The man turned out to be Roger Angell, the small woman Lillian Ross—a staff writer and William Shawn's mistress.

I tell the head of trade publishing at Prentice Hall that I'm going to leave. And like Carl Andrews a couple of years earlier, he gets angry. "You promised us at least two years," he says. "This is the trouble with young people today—they think they can just walk away from their obligations and break their promises. No sense of responsibility. You don't seem to have awareness of what giving your word means, and ... and I ... and"—here he starts to smile in spite of himself—"and if I were you, I'd do exactly the same thing!"

We part on good terms.

Twenty-seven to twenty-eight

The Checkers at *The New Yorker* sit in a room about fifty by twenty feet, on the nineteenth floor of an old office building at 28 West

44th Street, which bears, near its entrance, a historical plaque about the magazine. *The New Yorker* occupies the sixteenth and seventeenth floors (Advertising) and the eighteenth, nineteenth, and twentieth (Editorial). The editorial offices consist of some regular shabby rectangles off the long lunchmeat-linoleum halls and also many odd-shaped warrens. The aptronymic Mr. Knapp's office is under the stairs leading from the nineteenth floor to the twentieth. Adrienne Foulke, the head of the Copy Desk (and a well-known translator of books from the Italian), works in a small bay off the office where the other two copy editors sit. Mary-Alice Rogers, one of two collators, who take all the changes from various proofs and put them onto one proof, sits in a dog-leg alcove, at the back of which is Edward Stringham, friend of the Beat poets and master collator. You ask Mary-Alice how she is doing— proofs festoon her desk at all times—and she says, "Here I am, swotting away." The head of the typing pool works in a kind of glass cage within the typists' office. Roger Angell's office is a magisterial one on the twentieth floor.

What you do as a Checker is read a piece and underline the facts in it, and then check those facts against written sources, if possible, or on the phone—if, say, the facts emerged in an interview and couldn't be checked otherwise. The work is done, or should have been done, always in the spirit of trying to prove the writer right rather than wrong. In many cases, if two reliable sources are in conflict, tie goes to the writer. When the facts are right, you usually check them off with lines like this: / . So a checked galley column looks like it has cilia growing out of some of its sentences. Some Checkers use cilia that go like this, as already shown: / . Some others: \ . It may have to do with handedness. The underlining is also often individualized.

There's no Checking manual. You learn by doing, and by apprenticing to Phil Perl, the head of the department and a character, and by starting with minor content, like brief book reviews. Some Checkers use just a black pencil, some use red for factual land mines, some blue for assertions that lie in the DMZ between fact and opinion—like this very sentence, maybe. Some use more than one color, so that heavily factual paragraphs look like orderly battlefields or OCD action paintings. If you find an error, you cross out the offending word—"epinephrine," say—draw a line out to the ample margin, and indicate the insertion of "norepinephrine."

If you're certain that something is mistaken but the writer insists on keeping it, or if you absolutely cannot verify an asserted fact, you write "on author" in the margin. Sometimes the writer may try to persuade you to check something off instead of onauthoring it, but you resist doing so, because if a letter comes in pointing to an error, you want to be able to dig up from the stored files the proof with "on author" on it so that you can exonerate yourself.

Too many fact checkers, at *The New Yorker* and elsewhere, become proprietary about the pieces they check, and turn the process into a contest. I try never to complain about being overridden by writers and editors; after having suggested a correction that isn't taken, I just on-author facts I believe strongly not to be facts and let the letter-writing chips fall where they may.

Fred Keefe is the person who takes care of such letters. He works in a small office off a small office off a small office and is very thin, gray, and wraith-like, and has a reedy, quiet voice. Despite this ultra-mild demeanor, most of the Checkers tremble when Fred walks into our smoky den with a piece of paper in his hand. "Uh-oh, it's Fred," Phil Perl says. If it's about something I checked, I retrieve the galleys or revisions of galleys or page proofs and point to "on author" and, pridefully, don't much mind where the chips fall after that. Though sometimes a writer claims that I or other Checkers didn't insist strongly enough or didn't make clear enough that an error was made. Hah!, I say to myself—I told you it was norepinephrine, not epinephrine, and here are the galleys to prove it. I still have to be right.

A word about Fred Keefe, office man of mild mystery. The elegant sportswriter Herbert Warren Wind (the last name also being an aptronym)—who resembles Geoffrey Rush and always wears a penguin-looking vest—and Fred are good friends, to the point of raising homoerotic suspicions at the office. But then someone tells me that Mr. Wind makes passes at women. Who knows about these things?

When I first meet Mr. Wind, however, he looks me up and down—really looks—and says, "And what sport did *you* play in college?" I tell him that I played soccer and was captain of the Swarthmore varsity soccer team when I was a senior. I don't tell him that I helmed the team to that 2–10 record. (We had lost our two British players, Ian and the heavy-smoking Adam, and also a Ghanaian who was said to be the son of Ghana's police chief. He had come to Swarthmore in part to play soccer, only to discover that he was allergic to grass. Or so he said.)

Whether or not Fred and Herb are an item, *The New Yorker*, like most small, intense workplaces, produces many romances and more than a few marriages. A Checking Department colleague marries Richard Harris, one of the magazine's most important literary journalists. Pat Crow, an editor, marries someone who works in *The New Yorker*'s library, where back issues are meticulously indexed and clipped out and pasted into medieval-looking black binders alphabetized by authors' last names. Daniel Menaker eventually marries Katherine Bouton, an OKer (you'll see), who walked into the magazine's offices because she was passing by, told the receptionist she was looking for a design job, and was informed that the Production Department was all men but that she might talk to Mrs. Walden, the head of the typing pool—called, of course, Walden Pond. She is married to someone else at the time, but that doesn't keep Daniel Menaker from saying to her, as he walks behind her into 25 West 43rd Street (she is wearing hot pants; yes, hot pants), "That's Kathy Black. I'd know those legs anywhere."

Many of these connections break. More than a few are less than licit. Daniel Menaker and Katherine Bouton: thirty-three years and counting.

One writer, the aforementioned Lillian Ross, sometimes seems to play games with the Checkers. Just after I start my job, I check a Talk of the Town story that Lillian has written about a professor. One sentence has him wearing a yellow sweater (or something along those lines), and on the phone he tells me it was blue. When I call Lillian about this, she says, "Oh, you got that, huh?" Now, either she got it wrong and was making believe she had made the mistake on purpose or she really did make the mistake on purpose. To check on the Checkers. Either way, unpleasant.

So here I am in a tobacco-smoke miasma—with wrecking balls smashing into the walls of Stern's department store across the street, in that cult described five years earlier by Tom Wolfe, the leader of which is a small, demonically manipulative, and (I believe) self-loathing—but in some very important ways brilliant—man with a quiet voice and a nearly floor-length overcoat. The glamour of the place has yet to impress itself on me, although the Checker sitting across the aisle from me often gets phone calls from someone who, when I answer for the absent desk occupant, ends up saying, "Just tell him Twuman [*sic*] called."

I write notes, corrections, questions in the margins of endless galleys of pieces about staple crops—soy, alfalfa (by backgammon whiz and William Shawn crony E. J. Kahn)—or of Henry Spottiswoode Fenimore Cooper's Annals of Space, or of

Pauline Kael's review of *The French Connection*. "Sources disagree on the amount of alfalfa produced in America last year," I might write in the margin of a Kahn piece. "The USDA says seven million tons, while the Alfalfa Farmers of America says more like ten million." Or, for Cooper: "The tool used to tighten bolts on board the space shuttle is, according to NASA, a ratchet wrench, not a monkey wrench." For Kael, it might be "The movie's press release says there are eighty-six different New York locations used in 'The French Connection,' not seventy-five, but, then, it is a press release."

You enclose each note in a quadrangle or circle of its own, while the suggested changes, like "norepinephrine," above, or "Gustav Klimt" or "seventy-three per cent," float unenclosed and vulnerable to the editor's X. You circle periods and put circumflexes above the commas, as copy editors do. And make sure "per cent" is two words, because it's from the Latin *"per centum,"* according to Miss Gould, the mad stylist who reads *everything* but fiction and poetry, for adherence to house style, and who has recently circled "with James, Jr. at the wheel" because it lacks the comma after "Jr." Above her corrective second comma in the margin, she writes, in its own circle, "Have we totally lost our *minds?*" (Miss Gould turns myopic and deaf in later years and hunches over proofs looking like a zealous Cistercian, and once, when she glances up to see the boyish reporter Anna Husarska standing in her doorway, says, "Are you a man?")

The editorial process is exactly as elaborate as *New Yorker* readers would surely like it to be. The Checking proof goes to the editor, who looks it over with the writer, and then sends it to Collating, and Miss Gould's proof goes to the editor and then to Collating, and if there is an author's proof it will go to Collating, and Mr. Shawn's proof will go to the editor and then to Collating, and then Ed Stringham or Mary-Alice "I'm just swotting away"

Rogers will take all the accepted changes and put them on a single proof and send it to the Makeup Department, where Irish and Italian men—Johnny, Joe, Carmine (the very short boss there), Bernie, and the Irish fiddler Pat—are pinning the columns down onto soft green desktops and figuring out "ornaments" and the type runarounds they necessitate and newsbreaks (the funny bits, from any text source, sent in by readers, to be printed at the ends of pieces when there is space to fill) and rolling up and putting the mounted galley proofs in a plastic container and sending it up a pneumatic tube somewhere for revision, or as a final. Smoke in that room too. So much smoke everywhere.

From Makeup, the final proof, or a proof for revision, goes to Chicago. One of the guys in Makeup will say, "It's already in Chicago," and I say to Phil Perl, my boss, "It's in Chicago." I don't know quite what that means, but I like to say it. It's like Narnia or Atlantis. Chicago. Chicago is where the printing plant R. R. Donnelley is. Time, Inc.'s magazines are printed there, too.

Nothing can express the transience of most periodical journalism as eloquently as a lot of the writing I work on as a Checker. A Letter from Paris, by Janet Flanner, on what is special about *this* Bastille Day. A Letter from the Space Center, by Henry S. F. Cooper, about scientists' anticipation of what the first moon rocks will reveal. Just the anticipation of the findings, not the findings themselves. One of Henry's interviewees says they will prove to be a "blockbuster"—that seemed to be the consensus. A lot of facts in these pieces are wrong. (Miss Gould might well have circled that last sentence and written in the margin, "No sense? Facts can't be wrong?") If, for example, Henry Cooper says it's white, it may be black. If he says Neil Armstrong drinks tea, he may drink coffee. If he says there are 14,700 pounds of thrust, there may have been 741,000 pounds of pressure. It gets to the point where when I call some of the scientists Henry uses for sources, they sigh a little and settle in for a long, and generous, session of rectifications. But, to be fair, space travel does deal in pretty technical and minute detail, easy to get wrong. I will find out how easy when I do some reporting later on, among many other places in this very book, whose first draft referred to a friend and contemporary as having founded a magazine that began publication in 1855.

Oh, and about Janet Flanner: In one column she refers to a story by "de Maupassant." I dutifully check the reference and find out that it is an ignorance to use the "de" when mentioning this writer's name. I put the suggested correction on my proof, which goes to Gardner Botsford, Ms. Flanner's editor, who is also the stepson of Raoul Fleischmann, the Publisher of *The New Yorker*. Mr. Botsford *X*es it out. I make an exception to my no-pushback rule and tell him that all literate sources agree that the "de" is a mistake. I go into his office and gently restate the case, with some backup documentation in hand. "You are telling *Janet Flanner* how to write a *French writer's* name?" he says. "Get out of my office."

Speaking of errors and Gardner Botsford: At *The New Yorker*'s anniversary party, given by the Business Department every February—to celebrate the publication of the magazine's first issue—and widely disdained but always attended by Editorial, I go to remove what I think is a piece of thread from Mr. Botsford's lapel. My mistake. I'm right—it is thread, red thread—but somebody deflects my hand, thank God, and tells me that that red thread is the insignia of France's Legion of Honor, which the French government conferred on Mr. Botsford after the Second World War, for heroism during the invasion of Normandy.

But in contrast to these ephemera, I also get to work on many pieces that have lasting journalistic or literary value: John McPhee's dual profile of tennis players Arthur Ashe and Clark Graebner, Richard Harris's three-part Profile of former Attorney

General Ramsey Clark, Renata Adler's account of the abortive effort of Biafra to secede from Nigeria.

This last piece contains perhaps the most vexed assertion that I have to check in my two and a half years as a Checker: "Major Dennis Umeh, a thirty-one-year-old surgeon who enlisted in the army on the day before the war, said the hospital had twice been strafed and bombed by MiGs." Not only can I not confirm that significant fact about the hospital, it is disputed by the Nigerian government (of course) but also by the Red Cross and, quite surprisingly, by the Biafrans themselves, who had every reason to confirm the assertion whether it was true or not. And I can't track down Major Umeh. The sentence is allowed to stay in the piece, partly because it is a statement not by the reporter but by someone else and also because the author herself insists it is true. You might think that fact-checking is almost always a 0-1 operation—it's right or it's wrong—but this incident's ambiguities turn out to be not all that unusual and show how hot a spot Checking can be.

Renata Adler is very smart and tremulous. Essential tremor, I would guess. She has a famous gray braid down her back and is fidgety. She has a law degree and a little later on serves on the congressional Watergate Committee, which impresses me a lot. She tells me, once, that she became a writer in part because she wanted to know writers. A good reason and a bad one.

The New Yorker gets some letters about the Biafra matter, as I expected we would. Fred Keefe comes into Checking, and Phil Perl says, "Uh-oh, it's Fred."

When I need help, Phil lolls around the stacks, plucks down a book seemingly at random, opens it, often goes to the back (index), then flips through pages disgustedly, turns one more page, lazily digitates what I'm looking for, and wanders over to me with the fact in question safely, lepidopterously pinned.

Some of the books: *The Social Register* (surprisingly reliable), *Who's Who* (less so), *Jane's Fighting Ships, Grove's Dictionary of Music and Musicians* (superb), the venerable *Britannica* (good but often idiosyncratic and sometimes even argumentative), *Webster's New International Dictionary, Second Edition* (still the gold standard methodologically, I believe to the day of this writing, though increasingly out of date), the less respected but in ways still useful *American Heritage Dictionary,* the estimable *Chicago Manual of Style.* Altogether, it resembles an agoraphobe's conquest of the world to master these books, which contain the world, in their way, and to be able to be sure at the start of your journey that without mishap or missed connections you will end up where you are headed.

However consciously or un-, *The New Yorker,* a kind of Jonestown of the literary/journalistic realm, encourages in its employees an ethos of superiority, essentialness, and disregard for fad and fashion. Shawn himself, in his words and demeanor, appears to disavow any self-importance. He wants to be taken as a quiet, modest man who puts the greatness of the institution he runs above all else. This faux-modest version of occupational vanity, in combination with native timidity, keeps very intelligent people in the same, often dead-end, jobs for years, simply because they can say, in this modestly quiet voice, that they work for *The New Yorker.* Great institutions, so long as they are small, will often (a) eventually take themselves too seriously and (b) try to camouflage their pride with self-effacement.

Shawn always claims that *The New Yorker* does not and cannot, with integrity, try to attend to what a reader might want to read. We publish what *we* like, and hope that some people might want to read it too. This modest formulation of hauteur finds its best expression in a remark made by a Checker when the magazine finally breaks down and adds a real table of contents—as opposed to the almost microscopically small and cryptic listing that seemed on occasion to fly around and land obscurely in Goings On About Town. The real table of contents arrives shortly after I do, and the new feature has been kept a secret, and when we all get our First Run Copies on a Monday morning, a collective gasp of dismay goes up from the Checking Department. A colleague finally says, "This is just *awful!* How could we *do* such a thing." Being green, I say, "Well, don't you think it's a good idea for readers to know what's in the magazine?" She says, "It's none of the readers' business what's in the magazine."

There are seven of us, including Phil. Phil slops around the place in that lazy-looking and fed-up way, but as I've said, he knows where to find anything in the reference books that line the metal shelves. Occasionally a Checker, at wit's or initiative's end, will call out "Room at large!" and ask a question. Less than a week after I arrive at *The New Yorker,* one of my colleagues says, "Room at large! What does 'Angeleno' mean?"

"Someone who lives in Los Angeles," I say. I feel as though I've just passed a test.

"It doesn't look like there's a lot in here," Phil says, putting a tedious piece by E. J. Kahn about efforts to establish vocational schools in Micronesia down on my desk. Then he says, "Did you notice my shoes?" I say no, I haven't, and look down and see shoes with colorful layered heels, like alternating slices of Muenster and beets. "Wow," I say. "Those are some shoes."

"You like them, eh? Guess how much they cost."

"Gee, I don't know—must have been a lot. Seventy dollars?"

"Thirty-four fifty-nine," he says, heavy on the *f*'s, for emfasis.

"What a great deal," I say.

"Guess how much I paid for this shirt," he might say. It would be burgundy with a strange sheen.

"It's a nice one. Thirty-nine?

"Nope! Eight bucks. Canal Street."

"Wow! Very special!"

The second week I am in Checking, the phone on my desk rings and "Hello, is this Mr. Menaker?" a miniature voice says.

"Yes."

"Mr. Menaker, this is William Shawn."

"Oh, hi, Mr. Shawn," I say. "What can I do for you?"

"Well, there's a sentence in Notes and Comment about the number of troops who are in Vietnam right now, and I would like you to check that with the State Department to make sure it's right. It's from a news story, and I don't know if it's reliable."

The people on the Vietnam Desk at the State Department always laugh when I check the reporter Robert Shaplen's Vietcong body counts with them. They think the CIA feeds him inflated numbers. Jonathan Schell is writing powerful Notes and Comments against the war in The Talk of the Town while Shaplen is writing semi-apologias for the war in the middle of the magazine. Schell is one of the Harvard crowd. Shawn has hired three or four of his son Wallace's fellow–Harvard undergraduates — Hendrik Hertzberg, Schell, Anthony Hiss.

"Sure," I say. "I'll do that and let you know."

When I hang up, a few of the other checkers within earshot are staring at me.

"What's wrong?" I say to the person who sits across from me.

"You said 'Hi' to Mr. Shawn?" she says. "You don't say 'Hi' to Mr. Shawn — you say 'Hello.'"

Twenty-eight

One night, in the early-morning hours, in the apartment I share with Jerry Cotts, a friend from Swarthmore, I wake up terrified —

of absolutely nothing. It is a classic panic attack—racing pulse, cold sweat, terror like none I have ever known, except maybe for a foreshadowing of it on the lower level of Grand Central back when I was eight years old, and my general trepidation as a kid. But it *feels* like absolutely out of nowhere. You may think that the classic anxiety of certain kinds of New Yorkers, tending toward the Jewish kind, is a stereotypical joke, thanks principally to Woody Allen. But I am here to tell you that it is no joke, for any locale, race, or ethnicity. If someone you know truly suffers from what is now called a generalized anxiety disorder, it is fucking *awful*. Yes, the handling of such a person, in friendship or in love or in work, is best when it's sympathetic but matter-of-fact and even business-like. I know that now. I can do that now. Even with myself, on those mercifully rare occasions when the old panic approaches. But for pity's sake don't dismiss this affliction as a chimera or a ruse or a plea for attention or any of the other at least implicitly condemnatory assessments that so many so often make of it. It is all too real, itself and nothing else, and it can be disabling. It came close to disabling me for life. The prospect of lunch with a colleague was torture. Flying was a sentence. Social life an ordeal. It's no wonder that with Valium always on my person and the need to lose myself in something that would take my mind off this dread, I throw my energy into fact-checking so violently. I start psycho-analysis and keep the Valium in the shirt pocket over my heart. This goes on, gradually abating, for many years.

This terrible fear, which quickly and typically develops into fear of the fear, has to be in large part a delayed reaction to my brother's death, two years earlier, and an even more delayed reaction, perhaps, to childhood problems, and maybe—maybe even more likely—to the separation from my family in early infancy. In someone else, those events might develop into no trouble at all. But they do in me. And the work I have to do to deal with them convinces me, if I needed convincing, that the seeds of other people's psychological difficulties are almost always planted very early, that they often blossom hideously in youth, that it is the devil's own work to overcome or so much as moderate them, and that while they may be tamed, they are, like trumpet vines, like tenacious rhizomes, essentially un-uprootable.

It doesn't matter. Well, it matters, to me. But if there's anything more boring than analysis itself, it's hearing about someone else's analysis. I would not put any reader or friend through the details of my therapy, the first half of which was conducted by a decent, patient man, the second by a colorful and confrontational fellow who once said, when I answered one of his questions the way he evidently wanted me to, "Ah-hah! At last the penis goes into the vagina!"

So I am a demon Fact Checker, even when I start out, as "the drudge." The drudge is the newest Checker and has to work on all the pieces that no one else wants to work on—Concert Records, On and Off the Avenue. And with all the writers whom no one else wants to work with—Lillian Ross, Thomas Whiteside, "Audax Minor" (Gilbert Ryall), the Race Track columnist. And who cleans out the metal-wire box of dead proofs every Monday morning. And after a couple of years, they promote me to Copy Editor.

Thirty to thirty-two

Checking has its real-world aspects: trying to resolve conflicts (even if only vicariously) in the reporting of that selfsame Vietnam War (Shaplen versus Schell), phone calls to Columbia professors to check on misreported sweater colors, congressional records, *Jane's Fighting Ships,* and strafed/unstrafed Biafran hospitals. Copy editing at *The New Yorker* takes me into a more fugitive and cloistered world. You have to spend your days looking up that it is indeed "congressional" and not "Congressional," and other such fine points. When Bob Bingham says to me, "It has been decided"—as if by some plenipotentiary power that gains its nutrients solely from the passive voice—that I should learn copy editing, I have no real idea of what lies in store. This, even though my mother was a copy editor and even though Copy Editing, the office, lies just down the hall and through the nineteenth-floor elevator lobby and immediately to the right. I have almost never ventured into this warren in my more than two Checking years. I am also ignorant enough of office dynamics and psychodynamics to not realize how rare it is to get out of Checking and to have this chance, and how envious my fellow-Checkers may be. (Some of them turn out to be lifers and many others simply drift away. Later, one Checker, by his own admission a real Checking fuckup, drifts away into fame and fortune, in part by describing that factoid sub-world of periodical literature and his drastic shortcomings when he inhabited it—Jay McInerney, in *Bright Lights, Big City*.)

When an editor, any editor, finishes the preliminary editing of any piece, he—and it was always a he in those days, except for the fiction editor Rachel MacKenzie—sends it to the Copy Desk. Mr. Botsford, Mr. Bingham, Mr. Weekes (Talk of the Town), Mr. Whitaker, Mr. Crow, Mr. Knapp, Mr. Angell, Mr. Maxwell, Mr. Hemenway, Mr. Shawn, Mr. Henderson. Do you notice not only the gender but the ethnicity here, except for Shawn, who is Jewish, even if not by name? (His family name was Chon.) Copy Editing applies *New Yorker* style to whatever manuscript is in its hands and indicates how the piece should be set up. Title (Annals of Copy Editing, say, in 36 pt. Irvin), subheads (The Final Serial Comma and Its Discontents—I), body type (11 pt., 13½ picas), initials (3-line init. and caps—or caps and sm. caps, if the initial is the first letter of a proper noun or a name: "JAMES JAMES MORRISON MORRISON WEATHERBY GEORGE DUPREE said to his mother . . . ," etc. Within the text that follows you have to know how to set block quotes (9 pt.), poetry ("line for line"), newspaper-syndicate names, and so on.

A big black notebook beetles at us by our side, *The New Yorker*'s style book, long sheets of paper encased in plastic which have double columns of words and phrases and abbreviations on them. The book contains normal rules (numbers are written out in words up to and including one hundred, and above that numerals are used, except for the big round ones, like five hundred and one thousand) and marvellous eccentricities—like that one. The past tense and some other forms of "marvel" and "level" and other words like them get two, British-style *l*'s so as to keep the reader from reading "marveled" as "marveeled," I guess—as if the reader would. Some other style-sheet entertainments: "polo pony"; no hyphen in phrases like "well-heeled" if they occur in the predicate; the names of ships are set in italics; "girl friend," not "girlfriend"; "God damn it" or "goddammit."

Next to the Copy Desk is Collating, where Ed Stringham is dozing or setting his chair afire and Mary-Alice Rogers is still swotting away. Then comes an editor, Mr. Whitaker, his office a hoarder's dream of train schedules and other railroad lore. He is a big, Churchillian-looking man in his sixties who always wears suspenders, a Princeton graduate, gay, I think, who fancies himself an acerb. He edits a lot of the magazine's columns, including The Race Track, and himself appears in Talk of the Town stories as "Mr. Frimbo," a train buff whose doings are chronicled by Anthony Hiss, Wallace Shawn's fellow–Harvard alum, the son of Alger Hiss. Mr. Whitaker is also known as "Popsy." When I first started as a Checker, I rode down in the elevator with the to-me-then-still-terrifying Popsy and stuttered out something about the day—something about its being nice, I'm afraid. Nineteen floors went by in silence, and when we got out, we turned in opposite directions. Then I heard, in Popsy's petulant voice, "Young man!"

I turned around and said, "Yes, Mr. Whitaker?"

"Young man, just to say, you certainly have a way with words."

Next, on the short east dogleg of the nineteenth floor come the OKers, including, eventually, the aforementioned Kathy Black. These are sort of sub-editors who read the Final proofs of everything and ask questions, often important ones, as a fresh and very smart pair of eyes at the last minute. One of them—Helen—has tickets. That is, if a piece is closing and threatens to close late, she almost always raises a fuss, saying, "I have tickets!" Often she takes the tickets out of her purse and brandishes them. Are they the same tickets each time, I wonder, the ritual being so predictable. Are they tickets at all? I think so, because Helen does indeed love music, and going to concerts.

Thirty-two

"Who do you think you are?" That is Robert Bingham, husband to my cousin Janet, and now Executive Editor of *The New Yorker*. He slaps the letter I sent to William Shawn down on my crummy gray desk in Copy Editing. His eyes are blazing. "A member of the *junior* editorial staff!"

"Well, I was trying to say something about Reich's piece that would show—"

"I know what you wrote," Bingham says. "I asked what you thought you were doing."

"Well, no, actually, you asked me who I think I am." My mistake.

"A wise guy too, God damn it." (Or was it "goddammit"?) "You made this point on the copy when it went through, and we considered it and thought there was nothing to it. Now you write a Department of Amplification and send it to Mr. *Shawn?*"

"I didn't mean to be disrespectful. I meant it seriously." Charles Reich is the author of the best-selling 1972 book *The Greening of America*. A more recent piece of his, about demonstrators in Washington, ended with a sentence as silly as it was ringing about the American people versus the authorities: "After all it is our Constitution, not theirs." I have noted, on the manuscript and again in my now evidently incendiary letter to Shawn, that many in our government take a special oath—an oath that most private citizens do not have to take—to protect and defend the Constitution.

Never mind. Maybe it is our Constitution. Maybe it's Alex Trebek's. That's not the point. The point for me now is that I am in very bad trouble. It was not my place, as a copy editor, to make such a comment, and probably wouldn't have been before, when I was a Checker. I knew that, but apparently I want to stage my own kind of protest—and get in trouble with the cops. It's also true that I have not yet become a good copy editor, or even a competent one. I forget the final serial comma, I neglect to put a downward-pointing arrow at the bottom of a page that ends with a period, I forget to run brief, set-apart quotes into the body of the text, I let common misspellings, like "rarified," slip by, and so on. A few days before Bingham arrives with this blow of bad news, Lu Burke, an OKer and another vigilante in *The New Yorker*'s grammar-and-usage posse, stopped by my desk, showed me something I missed—omitting a pair of single quotes inside double quotes—and said, "You don't really want to do this work, Dan."

"We'll have to talk about this some more, you know," Bingham says at the end of this dressing-down.

He comes back a few days later. The white-haired, red-faced late-shift copy editor is sitting at his desk near the dirty window that looks out over rooftops and a crumb of Fifth Avenue. He keeps a flask in the top drawer of his desk. He has, with regard to the top of that desk, already declined from the perpendicular to the parallel. Asleep. But Bingham asks me out into the hall anyway.

"Now look," he says, "I'm sorry to tell you that we want you to look for another job."

"When?" I say.

"We're not going to make you leave," he says. "But we do want you to find another job."

"OK," I say.

"I'm sorry."

"Me too."

"You can take as long as you need to."

It takes twenty-six years.

I'm sitting at the Copy Desk one Tuesday evening, in the middle of 1973, waiting to copy-edit some Talk of the Town stories that are coming through late — waiting in general, too, to find another job, as one lead after another either disappears or presents prospects so dismal (writing and copy-editing a plumbing-supplies corporation's newsletter, for example) that I would choose unemployment and maybe even starvation before applying for them. Basically a ghost in the house. A utility infielder standing in for the utility infielder. As Johnny Murphy in the Makeup Department said of one of the other *New Yorker* haints, "Forgotten but not gone."

William Maxwell has sent down a short story by Sylvia Townsend Warner to be copy-edited, with a note saying "No rush." But oh, why not? I'll just have to do it tomorrow, and there is almost certainly going to be time to do it tonight. Mr. Maxwell always asks for the most minimal copy-edit anyway. Like just indicating font, indents, space breaks, and so forth. I have noticed that when writers really deserve this kind of respect, he respects their deviations from house style and rules. And, alone among editors in this way, he always wants the manuscript to go back to him before it goes to Makeup and on to Chicago. I've caught sight of Maxwell a few times, said hello when he stopped by the Copy Desk to hand over a story. He is a slender, long-faced, elegant man in his seventies with a quiet, almost hoarse voice, usually dressed in a gray suit. I hardly know him at all. But I can tell that he puts the writers he works with above *The New Yorker*—that he feels it literarily incumbent on him to do so.

Sylvia Townsend Warner's story is another in a series of fairy stories she has been writing—fantasies about small supernatural creatures who have human frailties and desires but also have some minor-league powers. Like the lesser Greek gods. I've found these pieces pretty forced in their whimsy. In any case, in this story one of the fairies "bridles" at something, but only in the strict physical sense of the word—rears back as a physical reflex. He or she isn't resisting anything psychologically, isn't indignant. But the way the passage reads, it's unclear that that is the case. The reader might plausibly think that the character *is* objecting, and at that place in the narrative, that impression would be, in a minorly serious way, quite confusing. I have nothing to lose, so I write a tiny note about this matter in the margin and put the manuscript in the Out Basket with a routing slip to Mr. Maxwell.

The next day, Maxwell comes down to the Copy Desk with the Warner story in hand. Who cares at this point, I say to myself. The worst has already almost happened. He very gently puts the manuscript down on my desk, leans over next to me, turns the pages until he gets to the "bridle" passage. He points at it and says, "If you ever want to do this kind of thing again"—oh, no!—"don't hesitate."

Thirty-three

I write a very short story called "Grief," centered on my brother's death, and give it to Mr. Maxwell, about whom a little more now. He is a well-known fiction editor and writer at the magazine and has worked with John O'Hara, John Cheever, Eudora Welty, John Updike, Mavis Gallant, and too many others to name or even count. My story consists mainly of a dream I've had recently about my brother's coming back to Nyack to visit, ringing the front doorbell, my letting him in. He sits down on the couch smiling a smile so white that it's frightening. He assures my parents and me that he's all right. He goes to sleep and we can't wake him up. But he finally gets up, surrounded by a dense, cold mist, and says he has to leave.

Before the post–Sylvia Townsend Warner invitation, Mr. Maxwell has occasionally thanked me for a comma or a capitalization here and there. His frequent overriding of *New Yorker* style—he does it more than any other editor does—impresses me.

Maxwell comes down from the twentieth floor once again and hands my story back to me at the Copy Desk and puts his hand on my shoulder, as if to steady me and himself, and with tears in his eyes says he thinks it's very good but too short and "needs something around it—a frame." So I try that and it's accepted and Mr. Maxwell edits it and *The New Yorker* publishes it. Writing it felt like releasing pressure from an emotional aneurysm that was about to rupture. It gave me a small measure of peace. I learn later that the magazine generally stays away from "dream" stories and stories about cancer, about the Holocaust, about putting aged parents in nursing homes. These subjects are either too familiar or too likely to overwhelm the human drama.

When it comes to the byline at the end of the piece, I say that I'd like it to be "Dan Menaker." Mr. Maxwell strongly urges me to use "Daniel Menaker." He says, "You're a professional writer, not some fellow who lives across the street." "Grief" is not the first thing I've written that has been published. A piece of mine about television-network news has appeared in *Harper's Magazine*. Another, about the PBS documentary *An American Family,* was in the *Atlantic*. I write these pieces in small part because I've always held strong opinions about television but mainly because I am watching it obsessively, as if it were not TV but an IV, a drug to distract me from my despondency and nameless fear. But when *The New Yorker* publishes that first story, I begin to think of myself as a writer. *The New Yorker* does that to a person.

My parents are proud. I hope that somehow the story has done more than just remind them of our loss—as if they needed reminding—but made something out of it, as it has for me. My friends congratulate me. My coworkers—I don't know. Some must be jealous. But it seems that the story is true enough in its feelings to affect many of its readers, inside and outside the magazine. My own publication reaction has far less to do with beginning to make a name for myself than with the relief of finishing something I had no choice about starting.

For a publication called *[MORE]*, a Seventies magazine about journalism, I write a piece about New York City's three local-news weathermen. They are Tex Antoine, Gary Essex, and Dr. (of Optometry) Frank Field. The editor at *[MORE]* sends the piece back to me with "Improve!" scrawled on the first page, and, on page three or four, "Make better!" I send it to the *New York Times*

Arts & Leisure section, they publish it, largely unedited, and the next day Dr. Field calls me and complains at length about "(of Optometry)."

Still halfway out of *The New Yorker*'s door, as an April Fool's joke I write a piece for the *New York Times* Travel section about a visit to the Royal Enclave of Schwindelheim, an (obviously) made-up nation-state that features, among other tourist attractions, the longest chain-link fence in Europe. I get three or four letters from readers who admired the piece and want more information about how to get to Schwindelheim and what other sites they should visit.

Thirty-four

The payments I get for these pieces and for the next couple of stories I sell to *The New Yorker* seem meager years later, but they don't seem meager at the time. My half of the rent for the shared apartment on West 75th Street is $75 a month. The one or two thousand dollars I'm paid for the first story in *The New Yorker* allows me to buy a wonderful old Gibson steel-string guitar, for a comparative fortune given my financial circumstances. My roommate and I sing those folk and union-song and bluegrass standards that have stayed with us. "Will the Circle Be Unbroken," "Keep Your Hand Upon the Throttle," "Join the CIO," "Long Black Veil," "John Hardy," "Roll in My Sweet Baby's Arms," "Dark as a Dungeon," "Wildwood Flower."

At *The New Yorker*, about as far from Appalachia as one can get, there are editors and writers and then there is everyone else. Most of us who haven't made peace with copy editing or fact checking for the foreseeable future want to be one or both of the former. There isn't much room, especially with so many desperadoes jostling each other in the halls as staff writers, and with editors, once they have landed in their coveted chairs, almost never getting up, and the other, aging Flying Dutchman types who grayly haunt the corridors hoping that a piece they wrote about Indonesian metallurgy two years ago may yet see the light of publication day.

At some point when I am still in trouble—this leprous period, this untouchability, lasts for about three years—I ask to see Mr. Shawn to try somehow to regain his good graces. I am sitting in his office, on the couch to the side of his desk. He turns his chair to face me. I notice that I have sunk way down *into* the couch, and although I'm about eight inches taller than Shawn is, I'm looking up at him. Tom Wolfe described this same subsiding-cushion phenomenon in his *New York* piece. After I plead my case, he says to me quietly, "Mr. Menaker, you could go anywhere else and be a . . . star." Distaste fairly drips from that last word.

Another time, with me still supposedly on my way out—and really and truly trying to find another job (I'm offered a position at the *Saturday Review*, but it folds the next week)—when I ask about writing a piece about Swarthmore, he says, "Well, I really don't mean to criticize you. I don't expect people, even the people who work here, to understand these matters and these distinctions. But what you want to write is an *article*, and *The New Yorker* doesn't publish . . . *articles*."

No diminutive has ever sounded smaller. There is a whole list of words Shawn hates, some of which someone has fashioned into this sentence: "Locating his gadget at the urinal, Tom Wolfe saw a photo of the intriguing, balding tycoon."

The women's-undergarment word "teddy," which occasionally appears in the column On and Off the Avenue, drives Shawn particularly crazy. "Isn't there some other word to describe this piece of clothing?" he asks in his tiny handwriting in the margin of a piece. He uses variations to register this objection repeatedly, as in "Can't we find another way to refer to this?" and "Must we include this word? There has to be a way around it."

I'm still working as a copy editor at *The New Yorker*. I've hung on, and since I started writing short stories and humor for the magazine, the authorities appear to be tolerating me instead of shunning me. This is Purgatory, I guess. I have just co-written and published "The Worst," a parody of a bestseller called *The Best*, a list book of the best stereo, the best wine, the best this, the best that. (Our Worst Wine: Switchblade; Worst Mammal: Jimmy's Tapir; Worst Ice Cream Flavor: I'ma Lima Sherbet; etc.) My co-writer is Charles (Chip) McGrath, who has recently arrived at the magazine as a copy editor. We work in the same crummy office.

For some reason, Chip and I are both in the hall just outside Copy Editing. Roger Angell, the best baseball writer in the world, the legend-in-his-own-time editor who works on most of the magazine's humor, and the hater of Goldie, Lillian Ross's little rat of a dog, is walking toward us with a pained expression on his face. He's holding a piece of paper in his right hand, flapping it up and down.

"Sorry, guys," he says. "I really hoped that something like this would never happen."

"What did we do?" I say, still on edge because of the trouble I got into earlier and my precarious position.

"It's just a rule we have," Roger says. "I'm afraid you have to return the payment for that humor piece." He flaps the piece of paper up and down some more.

"But why?" Chip says.

"It's just a rule—you couldn't have known about it. But you have to return the payment. I'm sorry."

"What rule?" I say.

Roger holds the paper still for us, so that we can read it. "The rule is that any writer has to return the payment for a first humor piece when the magazine receives a fan letter about it from Groucho Marx." He laughs.

Chip and I pass the letter between us. Roger goes away, chuckling. When we go back to our office, we decide to flip a coin for possession of the letter. I win. It says we're as good as S. J. Perelman, a writer I have never found funny, but by God I will take it.

A couple of weeks later, my roommate and I decide to find places of our own. The green parrot I've bought, whom I've named Edward J. Brownstein, after my analyst, is driving my roommate crazy with his squawking. He's also very proprietary about me and will attack others if they come near me when he's sitting on my shoulder. Ed is not a great talker. He imitates Readie's cackling laugh—since I've moved back to New York, Readie has occasionally cleaned our apartment—and he says, "What are you doing, Ed?" Which is what I say to him when I get home. And he imitates police sirens, at a distance, the way they sound from the street below. And, because I sometimes leave the radio on for him when I go to work, he says, "All news all the time."

Jerry and I flip a coin to see who gets to stay and who has to leave. I lose. I think, "I'll take the Groucho coin toss over this one any day."

More pranks: Pauline Kael, *The New Yorker's* movie critic, is always trying to provoke Shawn with her rowdy language. He has asked me to let him know if there is anything he—sorry: "we"—might find offensive in the copy when it arrives at the Copy Desk, so I sometimes have to call him at home in the evening when Pauline hands her column in late. If he has objections, he tells me to substitute "TK TK" ("to come") for the offending passage. So one night

I decide that I should call him about her description of a scene in which a man butts his head into a woman's crotch. It's mild, but why take chances when I am still on such shaky ground?

"I don't like it," he says. "Let me think . . . 'Vagina' wouldn't work." He pauses a few more seconds and then adds, "Because that's the opening."

Actually, he isn't the first to know about the crotch. When I first called, Mrs. Shawn answered. I said, "Mrs. Shawn, this is Dan Menaker calling from *The New Yorker*."

"Oh, yes, Mr. Menaker. How are you?"

"Fine, thank you. And you?"

"Fine. How can I help you?"

"Well, I'm copy-editing Miss Kael's Current Cinema column, and there's something in it that I think Mr. Shawn might object to, and as I think you know, he has asked me to call him under such circumstances. It's sort of marginal this time, but I thought I should check."

"Oh." A giggle. "I'm sure you're right—Mr. Shawn would want to know. He should be home very soon. But in the meantime, why don't you tell me what the trouble is and I'll tell him the minute he walks in the door."

"It's a little embarrassing. Maybe I should just talk to Mr. Shawn."

"You're married now, aren't you, Mr. Menaker?"

"Uh, yes."

"Well, then, I think it's perfectly all right for you to tell me."

After having those stories published in *The New Yorker*, I sign up with Doubleday to do two books, a collection of short fiction and then a novel, which is less a gleam in the eye than a tiny pinpoint of light, like that of a negligible star shed 400,000 years ago on whose very existence an astronomer at Mount Palomar has already cast doubt. The following year, the collection, *Friends and Relations,* is published.

"Daniel Menaker's stories in 'Friends and Relations,' trying very hard to be 1970's up-to-date, have a wearying sense of deja-vu about them ... These [stories] have ... certain twinges of feeling that—I guess—are meant to pass as Deeper Thought."— Robie Macauley, in the *New York Times Book Review.*

"Don't worry about it—it doesn't mean anything," a colleague at *The New Yorker* says to me, radioactive with Schadenfreude. "He's obviously jealous," someone else says. "It says more about him than it does about the book." "He's the fiction editor at *Playboy*—he just has it in for *The New Yorker.*" (This last is said sincerely, and just possibly with some degree of accuracy.) "Listen, most books don't ever get reviewed in the *Times.*"

One of the things I have to do as I continue to copy-edit and hang on to the cliff of employment at *The New Yorker* is make entries onto and delete entries from the "long-fact list." This list consists of all the major nonfiction pieces the magazine has on its bank, the top five or ten places on the list indicating priority for publication. We say "on" rather than "in" the bank for riverine reasons, I think; these pieces aren't in a vault but waiting to be launched and travel downstream to publication. (I've since learned that "bank" is an old printing term; it refers to a cabinet on whose slanted top galleys of type are stored, thus "on the bank.") In any case, the long-fact list grows for months at a time. Shawn buys more pieces than the magazine can ever run. I come to learn that payment for each of these pieces runs from five to twenty thousand dollars.

It's my understanding that on grounds of space and sometimes taste, *The New Yorker* turns advertising away in the fall, in the lead-up to Christmas. It does this because 248 pages is the limit for a magazine to be bound in the traditional way. If the writing and advertising pushed it beyond those 248 pages, it would have to be "perfect-bound"—have a flat spine with the pages glued, instead of being "saddle-stitched," a folded and stapled spine. Shawn won't allow this to happen. Nevertheless, the magazine's revenues evidently allow Shawn to buy too many pieces for the magazine to run, and then also to buy off their authors.

Every six months or so, when the list becomes laughably long—forty or fifty pieces or more—I get a directive simply to lop off about half of them and make a new list. They not only disappear from the list but also lose any chance of ever being published. So let's say I get such an instruction—am told to remove twenty of fifty pieces. That means the magazine is basically throwing away around $200,000. In order to try to contain the rage among those writers who have been strung along, sometimes for years, and whose work has now bitten the dust, Shawn often pays them still more—a kill fee, on top of the original payment for the piece. I believe the kill fee is about two or three thousand dollars.

As I've said, *The New Yorker* is fat with advertising, especially in the fall. This may explain how Shawn can follow his wastrel way of buying and killing pieces. I believe he believes that he is sustaining writers. As I am in psychoanalysis at the time, I begin to see how ultimately cruel and manipulative this practice is, how it doesn't so much string writers along as string them out, as with an addiction, and makes them dependent on one man's minimagus decisions.

Thirty-five

I have at last become a decent copy editor and, still like that utility infielder, am filling in at other, arcane *New Yorker* desks: collator (taking all the changes from different proofs and putting them on one proof, for revision); A-issue editor—not nearly so grand as it sounds (it just means reading final galleys against ads, to point out any "conflicts," such as an ad for a cruise ship running alongside a piece about a cruise ship's sinking); proofreader for the tiny typography of Goings On About Town.

Gardner Botsford, the great, WASPy editor who is the stepson of the magazine's Publisher and chief stockholder, Raoul Fleischmann, oversees the tiny type of Goings On. He tires of repeating the same copy for a long-running Broadway play and begins to insert, in order, short (blurb-length) passages from a novel of the eighteenth or nineteenth century. As a copy editor, I notice this small literary prank and like it. After a few weeks of doing this, Botsford drops off the galleys of GOAT (as it is called) and asks if I know what novel morsels he's purloining. For the first time, I look at the prose very hard for a minute or so and then say, "I don't know which novel it is, because this passage has no characters' names, but I think it's by Jane Austen." He's impressed. *I'm* impressed. Obviously.

Bob Bingham teaches me how to play squash at the Harvard Club, across the street from the magazine's offices. When he flubs a shot, he gets that eye-blazing kind of anger he had when he upbraided me a few years earlier—but comically (he thinks). He holds the squash ball in his hand, glares at it, loudly addresses it as "Sir," and berates it for its waywardness. Players on adjacent courts often shout at him to be quiet.

Some of *The New Yorker*'s other staff, for all their Olympian airs, fall prey to the squash explosion of the mid-Seventies. A squash ladder goes up on the nineteenth floor bulletin board. My closest rival (six years younger than I am, I feel a strange compulsion to point out) and I play once or twice a week at courts opened and owned by a writer named Harry Saint, who more closely resembles an upper-crust F. Scott Fitzgerald character than anyone I've known before or after.

I never lose a three-of-five-game set to this rival. And then I do. But my opponent makes his own mistake, the mistake of saying after the game, in the locker room, that I will never beat him again. If he hadn't said that, he might have been right; our games were always close and somewhat tense, given a similarly competitive situation at the magazine. But as he did say it, he never beats me again. The laurels a year or so later prove very comfortable to rest on.

The blessings of sibling rivalry's legacy. I'm still proving myself to Mike, and I will not give up, on the court or in *The New Yorker*'s offices. But the curses of it, too—the intensity, the absence of composure, the anger of competition.

It's at this age that I begin to understand what probably held me back from being a more accomplished athlete through high school and college. I just didn't have the confidence and the will that goes with it to practice hard and, most important, to *think*, because—well, because in some general way I was afraid. During my short and mediocre squash years, I find out what my high-school soccer coach, Frank Nelson, meant when he took me aside four or five times and said, "Danny, don't be in such a hurry to get rid of the ball. It's as though you're afraid of the responsibility or something like that. But you can handle it if you give yourself a little time to think about what you're doing. A lot of times soccer is actually a slow sport. It's a little bit like chess."

How much did I miss, out of haste, intensity, and anger? How much would I come to wish that I had learned about a quieter kind of effort and persistence earlier on, about winning for myself instead of proving myself to, or against, others? A lot. But how much did I gain from this single-mindedness and this same intensity? A lot. I actually did slow down in my thinking in squash—

a very, very fast sport. I actually did put my mind to copy editing and learn it; as you can see, I even mastered the semicolon. Later, in book publishing, when I wanted to get a quote from an important writer for a book I was editing, I would open my skull and tear my brain apart to find some connection to that person. And when, later, I faced medical challenges, I would try to become as expert in the illnesses and treatments involved as a layman could be. In one instance, when the doctors themselves weren't sure what course to take, I went against their first recommendation and may have saved my own life, at least for a while. "Look it up," my mother would say when I was in high school and asked her what a word meant. Eventually, when I get the more destructive and self-defeating elements of my competitiveness under some control, the kind of mild obsessiveness she was encouraging, the obsessiveness further developed at Swarthmore, blossoms into deep curiosity, and my intense focus serves me well.

The New Yorker's Business Department institutes a mandatory retirement age of sixty-five. (Mandatory retirement rules are still legal, obviously.) It does this, some people who should know tell me, in order to force Shawn to retire. But he takes the rule and tortures it into requiring everyone over sixty-five who is not a department head to retire. This little pretzel exempts him and Carmine Peppe, the head of the Makeup Department, from having to leave. But it means that some others, including three fiction editors—Rachel MacKenzie, Robert Henderson, and Mr. Maxwell—will have to leave. Mr. Maxwell tells me that he hopes and believes this turn of events will allow me to become an editor.

I don't know this at the time, but, as Mr. Maxwell tells me later, he goes to Shawn and agrees to leave quietly, provided Shawn gives me a chance to be a fiction editor. Apparently Shawn's twist on the business department's new rule opens him to regulatory challenges. In any case, Shawn agrees—how unhappily I can only imagine. (At one point earlier, when somehow I managed to discuss being an editor with Shawn, he said that I just wasn't a *New Yorker* editor, and that "no one can learn to be a *New Yorker* editor.")

Shawn calls me into his office. "It has been decided," he says, drawing from authority's auto-replenishing supply of the passive voice, "to give you the opportunity to be an editor. You have in recent months been very cheerful and persistent."

"That makes me sound a little like a golden retriever," I say—my mistake again—"but thank you."

"As you know, Mr. Maxwell will be leaving the magazine in January, so you will work with him directly, in his office, for three months, as will Mr. McGrath, who will also become an editor."

So here I am, apprenticing to be a *New Yorker* editor with William Maxwell, working in his office with him for three months. I'm the first reader for a story by Judith Speyer called "The Man with a Balloon in His Heart." I think it's very good and ask Mr. Maxwell to read it. He agrees, and *The New Yorker* buys it.

The story includes this passage: "You are an asshole. Your mother is an asshole. Your father is an asshole. I am lost in a den of assholes." Shawn notes in the margin of the galleys, with a tone of Homeric sadness, that he sees "no way around" using this word—another first in the magazine's history. In his quiet way, Mr. Maxwell clearly enjoys Shawn's discomfiture.

I work in Mr. Maxwell's office every day and leave only for lunch and when he takes his daily nap, at around one or two. We sit there, and together we read manuscripts that have been submitted to him, and I shadow-edit pieces that have been accepted and try my hand at editorial correspondence with writers. We go over the Checking proofs side by side, discuss titles, and review copy-editing suggestions about commas and typefaces and whether to run in a two-line quote from a poem or set it line-for-line in 9-point type.

It's all a little *raffiné* for me, though I admire and respect Mr. Maxwell tremendously. Or *because* I admire him so much. I feel out of place. I belong back down on the Copy Desk on the nineteenth floor, with Chip McGrath, who is also about to become an editor, smoking and making sarcastic jokes about the magazine's hoi polloi proofreaders and collators and its desperate writers, who wander the halls like Hades' restless shades. Or I belong out on the sidewalk, where they tried to throw me four years earlier and I hung on like a barnacle. Having struggled so hard to become an editor, I now miss being marginal and expendable, with nothing significant expected or wanted from me. I feel on the spot.

Why did I want to do this, anyway? To pretend to be mannerly, a person of letters, when I want to be a person of beer and cigarettes and impregnable skepticism? Isaac Bashevis Singer comes in to talk about the editing of a story he has just sold to us. Mr. Maxwell introduces us and says, "Mr. Menaker has made some small editing suggestions that we'll talk about when we go over the galleys. I hope you don't mind." Mr. Singer looks me up and down and says, "So young?" Bernard Malamud comes in for an editorial meeting and Mr. Maxwell introduces us and says, "Mr. Menaker has a couple of ideas about the ending that I think are worth discussing." I say to Mr. Malamud, "Please call me Dan." He says, "So soon?"

Finally, I squirm into a confession of this sense of unworthiness to Mr. Maxwell. One day, over tea — he has tea every afternoon — I say, "I'm not sure I'm suited to this. I feel like it's all above my head. It baffles me why you picked me out to train for this job."

"Well, I don't agree with you," Mr. Maxwell says. "I think you're perfectly suited to it. You know how to read like an editor and you know what it means to be a writer. And you dress for the part." He laughs.

"Well, thanks, but still, the atmosphere is so quiet and, well, *special*."

"What can I do to make you feel more comfortable?" he says.

"It's nothing anyone else does or doesn't do. It's me. I mean, if you had any idea how much I *swear*, for example, I think you'd be appalled."

Mr. Maxwell finds this uproariously funny. "Is that all?" he says. "We can certainly address that."

For the next few days, he goes out of his way to curse when we talk together. He isn't making fun of me or of what I said. He is genuinely trying to put me at ease. It doesn't work. It's just hilarious to hear this slender, elegant literary fellow, who maintains the most refined correspondence with people like Elizabeth Bishop and Mavis Gallant and John Updike, injecting obscenities into his casual remarks.

"You know, this isn't working," I tell him after a while. He has just said something like "Let's go over the fucking Author's Proof." "It's worse."

Mr. Maxwell finds this even funnier. I start to laugh too. He says, "All right — I'll stop. But no more of this fish-out-of-water business. You'll just have to take my word for it. You'll grow into it."

When I get to know him better, it turns out that Mr. Maxwell curses, naturally, a fair amount himself, in his own, delicate way.

Many, many years later, a dog, a Tibetan terrier, comes into my family's life. We name him Maxwell. A tribute or an insult? A tribute, as far as I'm concerned, because a dog figures in one of my fondest memories of the man. In Mr. Maxwell's novella *So Long*,

See You Tomorrow, based on a true story about passion and murder on a farm in the Midwest and published in its entirety in *The New Yorker* well after he has left, William Maxwell invents, for the purpose of witnessing some crucial events, a thinking dog. As in: "The dog took note of the fact that he didn't do any of these things." And: "The dog couldn't imagine what had gotten into them."

This thinking dog causes a stir in the Fiction Department at the magazine when the work is about to appear in its pages. Maxwell's editor is Roger Angell, and he and others of us in the department think that the thinking dog is a mistake. On several occasions Roger urges Maxwell to put the thinking dog to sleep. Maxwell is reported to have responded, in Bartleby-esque fashion, "I'd like to keep it." Roger Angell is not and never has been an easy editor to face down, but this is no contest. If you look back at *The New Yorker* issues of October 1 and October 8, 1979, you will find the thinking dog there, thinking away, to say nothing of taking note and imagining. He probably suspects that some time ago someone wanted to rub him out, and he may even pause to wonder why you're there checking on him.

William Maxwell is widely regarded as a sweet and gentle man. And he is—sometimes, in his writing and editorial sensibility and in his personal and social lives, almost to the point of preciousness. If you tell him that you have just taken your son to camp or that your wife had burned a roast the night before, his eyes may fill with tears. A few wiseacres at *The New Yorker* refer to him as "Waterworks." The atmosphere at the dinner table in his apartment on East 86th Street can be so literary and artistic that it seems to depart the hardscrabble world entirely. (Maxwell's wife, Emily, is a painter.) A lot about Tolstoy and two Elizabeths—Bowen and Bishop. The voices so quiet and modest that they can hardly be heard. And his taste in literature can be very special. For example, the way he loves those elf stories of Sylvia Townsend Warner. But he stuck by them until the end. In a letter in November 1999, responding to my teasing him about those pieces, he will write, "Your inability to get any pleasure in Sylvia's Elfin stories has driven me back to the book. I read the first story last night and was beside myself with pleasure."

So within Maxwell's delicacy there lurks a terse kind of assurance. In his writing, some of his sweet sentences and many of his neutral ones pull up short—end abruptly, even curtly, as if he were requiring his language and his own voice to return to plain speech and unsweetened reality. From "Over by the River": "A child got into an orange minibus and started on the long devious ride to nursery school and social adjustment." "He smiled pleasantly at George and watched Puppy out of the corner of his eyes, so as to be ready when she leapt at his throat."

More often than one might at first realize, the gentility of his style falls away altogether, and when it does, it reveals the frank and sometimes grim man who is always standing behind it and is perhaps using civility of expression in part to make more emphatic the awful shocks that—since his own mother's death when he was a child—he knows lie in wait for all of us. From *So Long, See You Tomorrow*: "Boys are, from time to time, found hanging from a rafter or killed by a shotgun believed to have gone off accidentally. The wonder is it happens so seldom." From "Over by the River": "If people knew how little he cared whether they lived or died, they wouldn't want to have anything to do with him."

In his conversation and his actions, Maxwell embodies this tension between civilization and its discontents, between the longing for a rational and cultured life and the bad luck and regrets and emotional anarchy that sabotage it. During those high-toned dinner discussions, when something difficult or bitter comes up, as it sometimes does, I can feel both Maxwell and his wife not only accepting its arrival but welcoming it. In a letter to me he writes: "Bad behavior one never really regrets in any serious way."

While I am training to be a fiction editor, working in Maxwell's office every day, I hand him some poems of mine, hoping that he will see the genius that resides in them but that others have always been blind to. Maxwell hands the poems back to me the next day and says, "Stick to prose." As an editor, Maxwell is similarly concise and efficient. He is in the office only three days a week but gets six days' worth of work done. (And he consistently takes that hour's nap every day.) He reads, edits, and responds to stories with remarkable promptness and unfailing courtesy and professionalism. Despite his sometimes rarefied literary inclinations, he is always open to strange and tough writing. And his editorial hand is the subtlest, least cavalier I will ever see. "Don't touch a hair on its head," he will say when I begin to scout around for ways to show off at the expense of perfectly good writing.

Unlike many editors, he feels that his first responsibility is to the text, not to himself or to the company that pays him. He is as distant from corporate as a cloud is from a clam and as far as I know has no use for office politics or machinations. In that way, in the way of the artist, he is subversive. And although he enjoys praise and gratitude, they never seem to go to his head; he never usurps the primary role of the author or congratulates himself or becomes puffed up about his sharp eye for talent or his eminent position. If he wants an editorial change and the writer refuses to go along, Maxwell never gets angry. He will give way but seldom change his mind. Once, when I am frustrated about an author's resistance to fixing an obvious problem, Maxwell says to me, "It's all right. Apparently it's a mistake she needs to make." Often, when the writer sees that Maxwell will give way, with grace, he himself will give way. It is an editorial version of kung fu—of winning by seeming to yield. But of course it is not combat; it's help.

Under Maxwell's tutelage, I learn not only to leave writing and writers alone for this reason or that—it's good enough, or it's a mistake she (or he) needs to make—but to temper my overall office impulsiveness. It's like a professional adjunct to analysis. Instead of getting into arguments, sometimes heated, with checkers or proofreaders, I learn to have conversations with them instead. At one point, Lu Burke, an OKer, says to me, "Dan, you really have changed. It's really noticeable." Since Lu herself is famous for her irascibility and disdain, I think, but do not say, "And vice versa, at least for a moment."

Thirty-eight

Members of *The New Yorker*'s editorial staff start a movement to join the Newspaper Guild. The magazine has given the staff skimpy raises for some years despite strong advertising revenues. Partly because of my mother's example, I'm sure, I am the only editor who signs a union card, meaning that I support the unionization of the staff, even though, as management, arguably, I can't be in the union. Roger Angell and other more senior editors remain neutral on the issue. (During the brief union drive, when someone laments that the magazine has no dental-insurance plan for its employees, Jonathan Schell reminds everyone, "Dostoyevsky didn't have a dental plan." And when we were all first arguing about joining the Newspaper Guild and I said to Jonathan, in my office, that I thought people who worked for the magazine ought to have some power over the conditions of their employment, he replied, "I'm sorry, Dan, but I can't continue this conversation when you use the word 'power' in any sort of connection to *The New Yorker*.") I am certain that they hope this event will finally lead to Shawn's resignation. He is in his mid-seventies now.

Shawn is not going anywhere. He keeps feinting toward this successor and that: William Whitworth (a quiet, smart Arkansan editor and writer), Jonathan Schell, Charles McGrath, and, ludicrously, the then-twenty-four-year-old writer William McKibben. When the staff resists these successor choices, why, then, Shawn has no choice but to stay on.

The union movement falters. An inevitably powerless Employees Committee is elected in its place.

When Shawn dangles McGrath before the staff as the next Editor—I'm guessing at least partly at Roger Angell's urging—he often works with Shawn in Shawn's office. Lillian Ross has her own telephone line to Shawn's desk, Chip tells me. And when that phone rings, he says, Shawn's face falls and his shoulders slump as if in despair. It begins to occur to me that this man is not only master of but slave to his circumstances.

The writing of my alleged novel for Doubleday has yet to get off—to say nothing of get out from under—the ground. I don't even know where to dig. So I write to my editor, Ken McCormick, asking to be released from the contract and enclosing a check for the meager portion of the novel's meager advance I've received. He tells me a few days later that he hasn't cashed and won't cash the check but has framed it and put it up on his wall, because it's the only time he can remember that an undunned writer has ever paid back any part of an advance for an undelivered book.

I marry Katherine Bouton. After having written and published two wonderful nonfiction pieces in the magazine, one about an archeological dig in Turkey and one about scientific research in

Antarctica, she has left *The New Yorker* to become a free-lance writer. Later, she will work for the *New York Times*—for the magazine, the book review as its Deputy Editor, the magazine again as its Deputy Editor, and finally the daily culture section. The people who work for and with her have great admiration for her editing skills and straightforward professionalism.

Katherine and I will have fertility problems when she and I try to conceive a child. We will undergo in-vitro fertilization, which will result in three ectopic pregnancies. Devastating. But we will adopt our first child, William Michael Grace Menaker, in 1983, and our second, Elizabeth Grace Menaker, in 1986. And in 2013, I say they are the best kids I could ever have hoped for, the old-fashioned way, in-vitro-wise, adoptive, or sprung fully diapered from the brow of Zeus.

As with almost all marriages I know, except for the one in a hundred that seem unvexed and therefore, to me, in a way not entirely real—maybe the ones in which the husband chronically and without irony refers to his wife as "my bride" and the wife refers to her husband as "my beloved"—we will have other difficulties. They will to some degree be caused by ancient problems, such as those old fears of intimacy, which will hurt my family, myself, and others. But Katherine is a rock of good sense and practicality and friendship, an excellent mother, and we endure, and we build a good and loving life together.

Thirty-nine

Susan Sontag sells a short story, "Unguided Tour," to *The New Yorker*. In it, a woman says, "I stroke my delirium like the balls of the comely waiter." Veronica Geng, Sontag's editor, tells me that Shawn has called her into his office to discuss this passage. According to her account, Shawn said, "Miss Geng, I don't want this word in *The New Yorker*, but I don't think there's any way to avoid it. Still, we owe it to our readers at least to try to find an alternative. So let's just take a minute or two to think it over." A couple of uncomfortable minutes passed. Shawn then said, "I don't suppose 'stones' would do."

Veronica, who is hired as a fiction editor a little after Chip Mc-Grath and I are promoted to the same position, says to me one day, about a writer she is working with, "Doesn't he remind you of Henry Green?"

"I'm not sure I know who that is," I say, having learned the kind of gentility so often deployed to disguise ignorance or hostility.

Veronica puts her hand to her mouth as if to cover a laugh of disbelief and disdain. "You're a fiction editor at *The New Yorker* and you don't know who *Henry Green* is?" she says.

A few months later, she tells me that a writer she's working with reminds her of the novelist Anthony Powell. She pronounces Powell's last name to rhyme with "mole." Actually, it more or less rhymes with "school." I keep my mouth shut.

Penelope Gilliatt, a writer and movie reviewer for *The New Yorker*, is found to have plagiarized certain passages in her piece about Graham Greene from an essay by Michael Mewshaw and from other sources. I'm present when one of the guys in Makeup, Johnny, hands copies of a new piece by Penelope to the subaltern who distributes galleys. "One for Checking," Johnny says. "One for the editor, one for Collating, one for Penelope, and one for the author."

I primarily edit fiction, but also some hoary columns, like Concert Records, which no one else wants to handle. Winthrop Sargent, former music critic for the magazine, has been put out to Concert Records pasture at least partly on account of his later reviews' intense and incessant diatribes against atonal music. His columns have devolved into almost nothing but listings of new classical recordings, their serial numbers, and brief comments. Very brief. "The Hindenberg Concertos, J. S. Wach. Vox Diabolique #ETC543210. Absorbing." "'Valse Manqué,' I. Bebusy. Canoli #UR666. Quite good." And so on. I have come up with three corresponding rotating subtitles for these columns: "Potpourri," "Grab-Bag," and "Miscellany." And I have written some more fiction and Talk of the Town and humor for the magazine.

And I work on some book reviews, one of which, by Robert Coles, offers a good example of the kind of heavy editing I and other editors often have to do. Dr. Coles is a renowned psychoanalyst. I had fact-checked his Profile of Erik Erikson four or five years earlier. When I'm done with the review, the first manuscript page looks like some kind of runic artifact or super-modern musical composition. It's so detailed and scholiastic that I herewith offer only the first two sentences as they appeared in that manuscript and as some of their contents appeared in the magazine, as an example of the heavy work that editors sometimes had to do.

So the first two sentences originally read:

> In the early 1970's the United States Corps of Engineers went about constructing yet another dam, meant to restrain an overbearing river. For a year before that sad and final turning point in the life of a particular American Midwestern community took place, a young writer and woodcutter, educated at Mars Hill College in North Carolina's western mountain country, came to an abandoned farmhouse in the soon to be flooded village and began getting to know the survivors, as they would soon enough turn out to be, of a place that had been for nearly two centuries home for many people.

And here is most of the material in those sentences as they first appeared in *The New Yorker*:

In the early nineteen-seventies, the United States Army Corps of Engineers set about constructing yet another of its dams, to restrain Caesars Creek, a tributary of the Little Miami River. This project required the sacrifice of the two-century-old Ohio farming village of New Burlington, which was south of Dayton and just north of Cincinnati; the town occupied the site of the reservoir that would be created by the dam's construction. During the sad and final year in the life of this Midwestern rural community, John Baskin, a young writer and woodcutter, lived in it, in an abandoned farmhouse, and came to know its inhabitants. He has turned the experience he had in New Burlington into an excellent book—"New Burlington: The Life and Death of an American Village" (Norton)—which is hard to classify.

As you can tell, the edited version, with the help of the answers to Checking queries that I put in the manuscript, introduces and relocates and untangles and puts off some factual material in an effort to present the basics of the book and the book's subject into more logical and less compressed—and less lamentational—form.

My actress girlfriend in our early New York days, when I was teaching at Collegiate, was taking classes at the Neighborhood Playhouse, under Sanford Meisner. She explained to me then the mistake of "indicating" feelings in performance. When you "indicate" while delivering lines, you show you are aware that you're acting and the audience will register the effort, the artificiality, of what you're doing. A lot of prose writers similarly indicate. They don't trust the facts and their objective observations to carry the weight of their attitudes and judgments. But they do carry that weight, as shown at *The New Yorker* most singularly and powerfully by John Hersey's "Hiroshima." This was one of the most operant editorial philosophies at the magazine. Some writers carried it to a mannered extreme, but most benefited from its application.

As I begin the work of editing, coarse and fine, I begin to understand the cliché "God is in the details." It's also the case that failed intentions are in the details, and confusion is in the details, and the unconscious is in the details, and camouflaged freight is in the details, and deception is in the details, and self-deception is in the details, and provocation is in the details, and surreptitious editorializing is in the details, and so on. God—if by God the agnostic means precision, clarity, genuine feeling, accuracy—is in the details only when the writer (or speaker, for that matter) knows himself and exactly what he is doing: rare.

Many *New Yorker* reporters have been more nearly informational than stylish or literary—E. J. Kahn, Elizabeth Drew, Robert Shaplen, Joseph Wechsberg, Philip Hamburger, Connie Bruck, Henry Cooper. In contrast to these stand John McPhee, Renata Adler, Jonathan Schell, Susan Sheehan, Bill Barich, Roger A., and, the greatest of all, Janet Malcolm. And many others. But it would have been impossible to fill a weekly magazine of many pages with original reporting that reached the level of literature; it took too long to develop those fancy pieces and to see them through to press. So the magazine had to have a steady supply of more pedestrian journalism and columns and reviews and brief reviews—and that stuff often needed a lot of editing.

Despite all this scut work, or because of it, with Mr. Maxwell gone I feel as if I'm still a little on the non-grata side of persona. A dog with bones occasionally being thrown in his direction. Waiting to fail. Especially in view of my having supported the union drive. No one is encouraging me, really; no one is shepherding me. Roger Angell does ask me to solicit translations of fiction by

Latin American writers, in view of the success of Gabriel García Márquez and the vogue for Jorge Luis Borges, whom the magazine already publishes. I do so. I keep a logbook of correspondence with and submissions by Julio Cortázar, Guillermo Cabrera Infante, Mario Vargas Llosa, and José Donoso and their agents and translators. One or two pieces seem to me right for *The New Yorker*. No one agrees with me.

Further: Maxwell accepted and published five short stories by me in a row—stories that were collected in *Friends and Relations*, the collection that Robie Macauley had so much grim fun with. After Mr. Maxwell leaves, my new editor, Frances Kiernan, rejects thirteen submissions in a row, over the course of three or four years. (She is titular head of the Fiction Department. I think her taste is generally questionable but pretty much right in my case.) I do manage to write some more humor for the magazine—parodies of Howard Cosell, Chinese Communist propaganda, a Zenish book about exercise, *Running and Being,* and so on—and some Talk of the Town pieces. But these successes do not succeed in making me feel less like the Pluto of the magazine's editorial solar system.

For instance: During a transit strike, I hitchhike around Manhattan and write a Notes and Comment about it for the Talk of the Town section. The last part of the piece consists of an exchange between me and a fellow–transportation improviser. "How are you getting around?" I ask him. "Diesel," he says. "Diesel?" I say. He points to his feet and says, "Diesel get me anywhere."

The piece appears in page proof the next day, a couple of days before Talk goes to press. The "diesel" ending has disappeared. I'm not surprised, as I know that like many people and publications, *The New Yorker* has a longstanding aversion to puns. But I thought this one was pretty good, and ironically aware of itself.

I submit an Author's Proof to Shawn which courteously asks

that the ending be restored. He calls me into his office and says, "Mr. Menaker, I see that you would like to restore the [pause] pun at the end of this Talk piece."

"Yes," I say. "It seemed to me to rise above the usual objection."

"I see," Shawn says. "Well—and I don't mean in any way to criticize you; you must believe me that this is not a judgment of you—you probably don't and can't understand why we can't do this. I really mean that—I don't expect you to know the full extent of the mistake this would be. You probably just aren't aware of it. But if we were to run the ending of this piece the way you're asking us to, it would destroy the magazine."

Forty

Max Frisch's novella *Man in the Holocene* appears in its entirety in *The New Yorker*, complete with drawings, diagrams, varied typefaces. It was submitted to me, and with the essential layout-and-design help of Bernie McAteer, in the Makeup Department, where galleys are still physically push-pinned down on gummy green desktops, I see it through to publication. It has been four years since I became an editor—four largely lackluster, pariah-like years. But when *Man in the Holocene* is published, Roger offers his congratulations.

A note from a reader, passed along to me, about *Man in the Holocene*: "Your issue of May 19th was a big waste of any reader's time with 72 pages given to that incoherent, irrational, uninteresting piece by Max Frisch. You alienate your readers by filling your pages with such trash."

How did the Frisch and how do all the other stories *The New Yorker* publishes find their way into its pages? The two stories we publish every week are chosen out of some two hundred and fifty submitted. So if, say, twenty-five of those submissions earn more than a cursory glance, then the acceptance rate from even that select group—of approximately two a week—is under ten per cent. So we start out with pieces that have arrived much closer to whole—and fine—cloth than are the often rough-woven assigned and pre-approved dispatches from the factual precincts of the so-called real world.

When a story comes in that one of us fiction editors—variously, over the years, Roger Angell, Charles McGrath, Gwyneth Cravens, Veronica Geng, Linda Asher, Pat Strachan, Frances Kiernan, and I—think has a chance or comes from a previous contributor and therefore might deserve a second look, he or she writes an "opinion" on it and sends it around for others to weigh in on. The opinions are sometimes called votes. Then, with the opinions attached, the story goes to Shawn for his final say. Here is a single set of opinions, denuded of all names except for mine and Shawn's.

To _____ from _____:

She's toned down the drinking—left some of it in but made it less explicit and kept analysis to a minimum—and she's given us a lot more of the two women. I don't think it ranks with her very finest stories, but I think she's caught the affection and need that characterize their relations, and the story has the feel of life. It occurs to me that a better ending might be "I reach to stroke him; he allows this, responding with a purr—and then is as suddenly gone," because there is something fragile about this . . . idyll. Any minute it could all fall apart. The story needs some fixing here and there, but it's the best thing she's done in a long time.

To _____ from _____ :

Agree. Still not much of a story, in some ways, but I think the writing saves it—it's natural and intelligent and always convincing. As you say, the best she's done in a long while. Agree also with your suggestions for the ending—or with *anything* that would eliminate the last paragraph. She means the reader to see through it, of course, but it's still flat, almost canned.

To ____ from Menaker:

The way the first twelve pages consist of phone calls and recollections still seems to me awfully awkward and slow, and though I agree that her having toned down the drinking a bit helps, I'm afraid that this time around the writing in the whole piece seemed to me at best workmanlike and at worst wooden, and I can't account for the difference between my reaction and yours and _____'s. I thought there were clinkers and hasty explanations and dead sentences everywhere—so many, in fact, that the story became tedious and hard to concentrate on. I'm sorry, but I just don't think we should publish this.

And, finally:

To _____ from Shawn [at the bottom of the opinion sheet, in his chicken-scratch]:

Sad to say, I reacted to this pretty much the way Mr. Menaker did. Also, I found it totally unconvincing. I'm very, very sorry. Nevertheless, I think Yes.

What? *Yes?* After that response? My paranoid fantasy is that Shawn has said yes *because* he agrees with me, if you see what I mean. Anyway, despite the atypicality of the final decision here, the opinions above pretty accurately represent the way the Fiction

Department works. There are prejudices, small amounts of politicking (back-channel conversations), favorites-playing, and so on, but the process stands in unusually favorable contrast to what will happen at the magazine later, after Shawn and his successor, Robert Gottlieb, leave, and what I'll encounter in book publishing.

Taken together, the opinions in the Fiction Department over the years will come to embody a fundamental difference in the literary responses of us editors. Some prefer what I think of as restrained and implicative dramas—the stories of Ann Beattie and Mary Robison, for example—and others, like me, go for more overtly dramatic and strange stuff. I think of "The Pugilist at Rest," by Thom Jones, the stories of Ann Cummins and Allegra Goodman, and the work of Michael Cunningham and Michael Chabon. But Donald Barthelme, unclassifiable, championed by Roger Angell, is the magazine's fiction magus. No one writing serious and accomplished literary fiction then or later will escape his influence. Even if you've never read a word by him or never even heard his name, he is in the air you breathe as writer of fiction. Same goes for Woody Allen and his influence on other writers of humor. Same goes for Lorrie Moore, I think. Same goes for some deceased authors who dwell in some obscurity for the general reading public, like Henry Green. (Who are today's Influence candidates? McEwan? Munro? Mantel? One is, for sure, Coetzee.)

Influence: My wife and I are renting Roger's house in Brooklin, Maine, near where his stepfather, E. B. White, lives. No kids for us yet. The bay's water sparkles. I recall a story Roger tells about Walter Cronkite's feckless efforts to dock at Brooklin. He is coming into the harbor and people are yelling "Hello, Walter! Hello, Walter!" at him. He waves, evidently cheerful about the recognition, as his boat runs aground. The people were actually yelling, "Low water! Low water!" Oh, yes: Influence. I write a piece of humor, a parody of Chinese Communist propagandistic press releases, called "Certain Questions in the History of the Party." I think it's probably just silly, but I show it to Katherine and she likes it. I send it to Roger and he loves it. Doesn't change a word. It's only when I see it in *The New Yorker* that I understand the Oedipally wishful, Roger-related, dinner-party-hosting subtext of the piece. And I wrote it in his house. Here it is, an interlude:

CERTAIN QUESTIONS IN THE HISTORY OF THE PARTY

BEFORE COCKTAILS

Despite the clarity and correctness of the invitation issued by our host, Moo Ving-van, for seven, Mr. Bo Tai and Mrs. Bo appeared at six-thirty, throwing matters into discontent and confusion at the outset. However, at that time, as at so many times before, Moo was able to temper principle with pragmatism, and gave Bo and Mrs. Bo productive things to do, such as arranging the canapés correctly and helping Moo to devise a seating plan for dinner which would maximize pleasant conversations and simultaneously distribute the party's two left-handers to his right and the right of Mrs. Moo. This strategy, which had been pioneered by Moo, helped to avoid contention and "kept a lot of peas off the floor."

Also, Moo put some beer in the cooler and filled the ice bucket with ice for mixed drinks while Mrs. Moo set up the croquet course and, with the help of Mrs. Bo, generally tidied the house, so as to accomplish what Moo called "getting everything really ready before the guests arrive." Unfortunately, Moo was unable or unwilling to take similar foresighted steps to check Mrs. Moo's flirtism, which, as we can see now, had recently been undermining his judgment and proved "to be very bad" for the party.

BEFORE DINNER

At seven, Moo welcomed Mr. Don Wenow and Mrs. Don, and made a completely correct introduction of Don and Mrs. Don to

Mr. Bo Tai and Mrs. Bo, since they all "seemed more than few feet up in the air" about whether they had met before. Don overcame a brief moment of difficulty in "starting things off in a good way" by initiating a discussion of ridiculism in mortgage rates. It was clear even at this early stage that Don was utterly devoted to the success of the party. The humorous twins Mr. No Go and Mr. No Weh arrived next, and after they were carefully and accurately introduced by our respected host, Mr. No Weh said, "It is a much more difficult task to tell us apart than to tell us the location of the bar," which caused some big groans and "kept things rolling in a great manner." Then came Mr. Hai Enlo and Mrs. Hai and their elderly cousin, Mr. Ah Choo; the writer Mr. Hao Yubin and his most recent fiancée, Miss Shi Zaten; Mr. Mee Omai and Mrs. Mee, from next door; and the young schoolteacher Mr. Ti Fatoo and his wife, Ms. Hoo Mi, who practiced the approved social variationism of retaining her maiden name. Miss Dun Merong, who lived in the city and was the last to arrive, explained that she had taken several incorrect turns.

Moo picked up the thread started by Don and steered the course of many conversations toward real estate. This was in principle the right thing to do for that phase of the party, but Moo could not seem to "leave it alone and change the subject in a subtle fashion," thus committing the error of monotonism and trying arbitrarily to impose his personality on the development of the party. The drinks were correctly mixed, the Bucheron was entirely without the taint of the barnyard, and the Kavli Flatbrød was crispily fresh. Thus Moo made vital contributions to the party, rectifying, for instance, the stoned-wheat-thinism that characterized so many previous parties, and for these and his numerous past contributions we revere and respect him to this day. But his prying questions to Miss Dun Merong about what she paid for her co-op on West End Avenue in '78 and his interruption of the croquet match between the Mees and the Hais with repeated invectives against owner financing subverted the party, despite all of Mr. Don Wenow's efforts to "close the lid on that one and try some pickles from another jar." Mrs. Moo analyzed the stalemate for her own purposes, drawing the young school-teacher Mr. Ti Fatoo into the kitchen, where she tried to arrange a private party with him for a later date. The end result of these bad, incorrect, and wrong errors was that Moo neglected to ignite the charcoal in a timely fashion, forcing his guests to endure the Long Wait for dinner.

AT DINNER AND AFTERWARD

The meal itself progressed along a basically admirable line — avocado vinaigrette, steak, shoestring potatoes, cucumber salad, and a muscular Burgundy. But Moo became increasingly difficult and capricious in his conversation and behavior. Mr. Don Wenow, by making a graceful transition between group-occupancy restrictions and *Animal House,* at last managed to switch the topic from real estate to movies — a fully acceptable topic for any party. However, perhaps because he became aware that Mrs. Moo was attempting to commit serious leg and feet errors with Mr. Ti Fatoo, Moo spoiled matters here again by "a big failure to realize that he wasn't a four-year-old." He cackled in a rude manner at the opinions of others, and then became morose about being forbidden to attend movies as a child. When others, led as always by the dedicated Mr. Don Wenow, tried to "get off the bus and go their own way," Moo atrociously butted in with more tales of childhood deprivations, and denounced his father, Mr. Moo Cao, for being too proud and severe to make enough money, and for never playing catch with him in the back yard. Finally, in a desperate attempt to keep himself at the center of things, Moo indulged in clownism, playing foolish tricks with his silverware and, during coffee and dessert, tossing grapes up and catching them in his mouth.

These discourtesies gave rise to the notoriously embarrassing Six-Minute Liqueur, after which the guests "fled from the wreckage in a quick manner," leaving Moo sullen and withdrawn. Mr. Don Wenow convened the intelligently strategic and now famous Meeting on the Sidewalk Outside Moo's House, and, ever loyal to Moo, explained to the others that perhaps his friend and teacher had given one party too many, and that Mrs.

Moo's liaisonism might be the cause of Moo's mercurial actions. While not exonerating Moo for his mistakes, Don reminded us again that in the past Moo had blazed the trail in many party areas and had straightened out a large number of errors, such as charadism, fondueism, and hosts getting up in the middle of the meal and "fiddling with the dimmer in an ostentatious way."

This analysis was so correct and balanced that it gave us a whole lot of understanding of Moo and a good perspective on his contributions and failings. In the new spirit of things, Don invited everyone to join him and Mrs. Don for what he called "a late breakfast" a week from the following Sunday, thus advising us "in a gentle and easy-to-take style" to reject brunchism, and at the same time obtaining agreement that the next party would be his.

Influence again: gently. I've had those thirteen consecutive stories turned down by the magazine since Maxwell left. That same summer vacation in Brooklin, I write another "clever" and callow short story, which Katherine reads. She says, gently, "You know, you can go deeper than this. You have real feelings, like everyone else. The story is smart enough, but I don't know—you could make your writing more honest in its emotions." It works.

Forty-one

Speaking of opinions, or at least opinionating, when I edit Pauline Kael's column, I have to go down the stairs from the twentieth floor to the eighteenth and take her a proof with my suggestions on it. A fan is always on in her office, even in the depth of winter, and it blows directly on her and me as we go over her piece. I learn a lot about "voice" from her. At the beginning of our work together, she would see my changes, often having to do with some sort of illogic, because she spilled out her prose in such a headlong and heedless way, and she would read them aloud and say, with uncharacteristic politeness, "That's elegant, Dan, but it doesn't sound like me, really." Then she would take the essence of the suggestion and render it into pell-mell Paulinese.

I learn after a while to make my suggestions in language closer to her own, and it helps me realize that *I* have a voice—this here voice, for what it's worth—too. And that every writer has one, and the more distinctive *and* natural—like complexity and unity, two qualities in tension—it is, the better it is. And she is for the most part very, very good.

As I came to understand as a copy editor, she also enjoys her side of the war between herself and Mr. Shawn. She bedevils him with risqué language and descriptions for the sole sake, I often think, of making gleeful fun of him when his proof arrives and we go over it. And she also furnishes me with a running commentary on the magazine's other writing. "What do you think of Notes and Comment this week, Dan?" she may ask.

"I thought it was—"

"It's soft," she says. "It's really soft. The whole magazine is soft this week. I hope it gets *hard* again soon."

Going to screenings with her can be embarrassing. They are usually held in small screening rooms, and everyone's behavior is on display to everyone else, and a professional silence and efficiency prevail. You go to the screening, you nod to a few people you know, you sit, you watch, you leave. But if Pauline finds a movie or any part of a movie absurd, as she does once with all of Luchino Visconti's *Ludwig*, about the degenerate life of Ludwig of Bavaria, with me in tow, she chortles and exclaims: "Oh, no!" "Oh, that's just awful." "I can't believe this." "This is ridiculous!"

She tells me that if she seriously disagrees with someone about three movies in any given year, it's hard for her to remain friends with him.

When my wife and I adopt our second child—our daughter, Lizi (Lizi's spelling, believe me)—and I tell Pauline about it, she is upset. Actually affronted. She looks at me angrily and says, "Now why would you do that?" I think my increasingly divided attention—which may have caused Pauline to respond this way to Lizi's arrival—leads to what happens next.

One day, after I have worked with Pauline for quite a while, Mr. Shawn suddenly appears in my office. He asks, "May I sit down?" (oh, honestly!) and then says, "Now, don't be upset, Mr. Menaker. I want to assure you that this is no reflection on your work. You have done good work with her and lasted longer than three or four other editors have lasted with her."

At this point, since it was out of the blue, I have no idea what or whom he is talking about.

He goes on: "You lasted longer with her than Mr. Botsford did, you lasted longer with her than [someone else; I forget] did. Why, you even lasted longer with her than I did." A small, unconvincingly reassuring chuckle.

I still don't know what he's talking about.

"But Miss Kael feels you may not have the time to work closely enough with her as her editor and would like to work with someone else."

About half an hour after Shawn leaves my office and I'm done stewing over how I've failed, I feel a great weight lifting off me. No more stairs from twenty to eighteen to twenty, no more icy fan air, no more whole-column recitatives, no more embarrassing screenings, no more crossfire between Pauline and Shawn. For a while she got from me what she needed, and I learned a great deal about writing from working with her, and so the bad is gone, the good remains.

A real liberation, it turns out to be, and a lesson about looking at failure from a different angle.

• • •

I'm visiting Mr. Maxwell at his apartment and talking to him about why writers write. The *Paris Review* has just published an interview with him, conducted by John Seabrook, in which he says that writers generally write out of a sense of deprivation—emotional deprivation, I think he means. In his case, the specific depriving was the death of his mother, when he was a young boy. I ask him what he thinks writers hope to gain by addressing a sense of loss by writing. He says, "Attention, love, approval. The attention they feel they missed when they were young. This usually means attention from parents. It may not appear to be a serious matter to anyone looking in on the family from the outside, but to the child involved, who may be a particularly sensitive child by nature, it is serious."

Finally on surer ground at *The New Yorker*, in part thanks to Frisch and getting in some pieces by Stanisław Lem, the Polish writer of idea-rich science fiction, I begin to understand how lucky I was in my education, from grade school to college to graduate school in English at Johns Hopkins—or, as Lyndon Johnson called it, when the university gave him an honorary doctorate in 1966, "John Hopkin."

The Little Red School House was marvelous. (Three of its alumni—Tom Hurwitz, Angela Davis, and Elliott Abrams—were the subject of a recent book called *Little Red*, by Dina Hampton.) The teachers, many of them no doubt Communists, seemed to think they were educating children who would become the intellects of the Revolution, and they did their teaching with missionary zeal. And the professors at Swarthmore and Johns Hopkins were of the highest caliber.

So I set about thanking some of them, including Sam Hynes,

who kindly wrote back to me, "And thank *you* for all you have achieved." And the madman professor of Romantic Poetry at Hopkins, Earl Wasserman. He had that monomaniacal subject-object interpretation of the main theme of the works of Coleridge, Shelley, Byron, Keats, and Wordsworth. Well, I mean, isn't all art ultimately about subjects and objects? Never mind, though.

Wasserman was a wonderful, crazy teacher, with a thick face, glasses, salt-and-peppery hair, and a deranged intensity. But he taught the closest possible reading and parsing of every word, phrase, sentence, stanza. It was humanities microscopy, and I realize that it has contributed significantly to whatever editing abilities I have.

So I write him a letter from *The New Yorker* thanking him for his valuable lessons in intellectual passion and verbal precision. He writes back something along these lines—I have misplaced the note: "Dear Mr. Menaker, As I recall you did quite a good paper about George Gissing's novel 'New Grub Street' for Professor Miller's class in Victorian fiction. And I see from your magazine letterhead that that is exactly where you ended up. Sincerely, Earl Wasserman."

Forty-two

I tell my analyst about seeing my mother's footprints on the ceiling at Barrow Street when I was four. He asks me, in his thick Spanish accent, "And why do you suppose this memory has estayed in your memory so vividly?"

"I don't know," I say. "It must have been pretty weird for a four-year-old to see footprints on the ceiling and then be told that his mother could fly."

"Who is this four-year-old you espeak of?"

"Me. What do you mean?"

"Oh, I see — you are Richard Nixon now, referring to yourself in the third person."

"Well, I *was* four, you know — hardly the person I am now. I seem like a stranger to myself at that time."

"But not so much a stranger that you do not remember this incident and claim it as your own, before you then disclaim it grammatically."

"What's your point?"

"Well, there is a reason you recall this with esuch intensity and then disown it."

"What is it?"

"This is for you to discover, but I will give you a clue. Did women wear eslacks back then?"

"How should I know? I guess not."

"Especially not at a party, eh?"

"I guess not."

"You have now run out of guesses. So how did those footprints appear on the ceiling?"

"They held her upside down."

"Yes, and what was she wearing?"

"I don't know. A dress, a skirt."

"Yes, a dress, an eskirt. And what might happen under these circumstances?"

" —— "

"Oh, for the good Christ's sake, I will tell you. You were unconsciously fearful and hopeful then, as you are now, that her dress might have fallen down and people could look at her poosy, which is what you wanted to do too. This is why you disowned it, like Nixon."

Many such exchanges with this mad genius of an analyst finally begin to make clear to me the unusualness, the unfortunate-ness, and the fortunateness of the romance between my mother and her two sons. My brother separated himself from it. But here I was doing her kind of work. You don't hear "in his mother's foot-steps" very often. It wasn't only bad high-school science teaching that kept me from wearing the stethoscope I might have worn, and it wasn't only the hardships of a musician's life that kept me from taking up the fiddle in a serious way, which I so longed to do.

Forty-three

We are on vacation in Truro, on Cape Cod, my wife and I, when the call comes from the adoption agency. We get ready to go, tell a crusty neighbor lady about why we are leaving, and she says, "Oh, well, that's all right, I guess. Someone in the village adopted a child from the Orient a few years ago. She's perfectly nice but a boxy little thing."

We fly down to Atlanta, and as we walk into the agency's of-fices, we pass a bassinet with a remarkably small person fast asleep in it. I think nothing of it. When we sit down in the social worker's office, I say to myself, "That is our son!" He is.

We live at 324 West 83rd Street, on the top (seventh) floor of a co-op with three small bedrooms and a nano–maid's room. We have an au pair. I go down to *The New Yorker*'s offices every day; my wife works as a free-lance writer. When Will is five or six months old, he's sitting in his high chair in the kitchen, messing with his food. I drop a raw egg on the floor and of course it breaks. I lean down to clean it up and I hear this strange *Gremlins*-type giggle. It's Will, the first laugh of his that I've heard; he's beginning to en-joy the human comedy and my mistakes.

· · ·

I write a much longer story based on the events surrounding my brother's death. Mr. Maxwell is long gone. *The New Yorker* turns it down. Chip McGrath comes into my office and says, "You really got rooked. It's a great story." My assistant at the time, a mischievous young woman, asks if I want to covertly see the opinions, and I say no. A few days later, she hands me a story from the slush pile and asks me to read it. After a couple of pages I'm mystified about why she would recommend such a clearly amateurish piece, but then I find that the third page of the story is not the third page of the story but the opinions on *my* story. I can't keep myself from reading them. My editor, Fran Kiernan, has written a negative opinion, Veronica Geng calls it "just another hospital story," and Shawn says, "I'm afraid I agree with Ms. Geng—just another hospital story."

A few months later, my friend Ben Sonnenberg, who has started a handsome and distinctive literary quarterly called *Grand Street*, publishes the piece under the title "Brothers."

I tell my analyst about the opinions on my story and my placing it at *Grand Street*. Instead of responding to the umbrage I've taken, he tells me that Mike's death is threatening to turn into a "nuclear integrative fantasy" for me. Nuclear because it is becoming the center of my unconscious emotional life. Integrative because it creates a shape, a terrible and beautiful structure, for everything in my life that came before it and has happened afterward. And a fantasy because for reasons of unconscious conflict and patterns, I've begun to inject its occurrence into many parts of my history upon which it has no rational bearing. He says that Holocaust survivors often present the strongest examples of this kind of centripetal emotional distortion. ("And who can blame them?" he adds.) Their experiences during that time shape everything that has happened to them, not only during the ordeal but before and after it. No transaction will ever be free of its dark power as long as they live. When he tells me about this, it immediately calls to mind a girl I'd flirted with at a bar, the Ninth Circle, in the Village, the college summer I worked in the Morgue—as Editorial Reference used to be called—at Time, Inc. She was pretty and nice but seemed dissociated. She excused herself for a few minutes just after we started talking, and the bartender said, "Be careful with her—her brother died three years ago, and it seems like it made her really crazy. She comes in here all the time and talks to people about it." And sure enough, when she came back, she sat down and took out a pen and wrote on a napkin, in very small letters, "My brother died," and gave it to me.

Forty-four

William Whitworth, the wonderful writer and editor, and one of Shawn's never-going-to-happen potential successors, inherits Pauline Kael, lasts longer with her even than I did, develops a stomach ulcer, and ultimately leaves to become the Editor of the *Atlantic*.

Forty-five

Natacha Stewart, whose work I edited at *The New Yorker* briefly—an inheritance from William Maxwell—dies. Pierre Leval, a United States District Court judge, holds a memorial/reception in her honor at his apartment on Park Avenue. Someone tells me about it, and I feel I should attend. I do so, only to discover that the event is by invitation only. I apologize to the host, explain my mistake, and he graciously insists that I stay.

I talk with Mrs. Shawn—Cecille, but of course I call her Mrs. Shawn. We're talking about something interesting. After a few minutes, she looks at her watch and says she's sorry but she should be going. I protest: "Let's just finish this one question," I say. She says, "Mr. Menaker, you don't understand. I really must be going."

She leaves. A short time later, Shawn and Lillian Ross arrive.

Not long before this incident, Alice Munro submitted a story that included an adulterous man leaving his lover's bed and immediately making a phone call to his wife. As I recall, Shawn wrote in the margin, in his tiny hand, that he found this part of the story hard to believe—completely unconvincing.

Under the heading "1983 Incentive Stock Ownership Plan," The New Yorker Magazine, Inc.'s, Notice of Annual Meeting of Stockholders, to Be Held March 22, 1983, stated that grants of stock will be made to certain employees. "All key executives and key employees of the Company shall be eligible to participate in the Incentive Plan ... The Incentive Plan will be administered by a committee appointed by the Board of Directors ... which will select the key executives or employees of the Company ... to whom awards will be granted." I noticed or heard about this stock plan, and after a couple of years I begin to wonder why (as far as I know) "key" Editorial employees weren't being designated for these grants. I go to the President of the magazine, J. Kennard Bosee, down on the sixteenth or seventeenth floor, where the Business Department is in effect pre-infatuation Thisbe to Editorial's Pyramus, and ask him about this situation. He tells me that Shawn has refused to name any key Editorial employees for these grants because the writers who aren't employees, even those under contract, aren't eligible. (It turns out that the same annual report, on page 14, describes the "1983 Authors and Artists Under Contract Stock Purchase Plan," but a stock purchase, however advantageous the price, is not a stock grant.) I say, "But isn't he *required* to designate key employees?" Bosee says, "He just refuses."

Shawn gets wind of my descent to seventeen and my concern and calls me into his office a few days later. He explains. He says he couldn't in conscience designate key employees for stock grants because most of the artists and writers couldn't have them. "And after all, they are the most important people," he concludes. I say, "But it wouldn't *hurt* the artists and writers if Editorial employees received these grants." I'm thinking that there must be some fairy tale or Aesopian narrative that illustrates the ridiculosity of depriving, say, the donkey of hay simply because the horse can't have any. But I can't come up with it. Shawn says, "Well, I don't expect you to understand this, Mr. Menaker, but it *would* hurt the artists and writers. This inequity would hurt everyone." I tell him that I disagree with him, that I think this isn't the right thing to do, and I think I even say something crass, like "Why not just get the money up here and we'll *all* split it up?" (What I wanted to say and didn't was "Isn't this at the very least violating the rules of the Securities and Exchange Commission?" Because it seemed to me that that might very well be the case.) And he just looks at me with this dyspeptic expression and I leave, and do and say nothing more about it. Later, when S. I. Newhouse buys the magazine, I estimate, approximately and conservatively, that the stock grants I and some of my colleagues might have received would have been worth between $100,000 and $200,000 for each of us.

I am still in analysis at the time, and when I tell my . . . colorful analyst this story, he goes nuts. "What is *wrong* with you people?" he practically yells. "Are you *sheep?* What kind of insane asylum are you working in? You should be not on this couch but down at the courthouse with a lawyer esuing this man Shown and even having him arrested! This is a cult!"

S. I. Newhouse, the scion of a newspaper millionaire and owner of Random House, has just acquired *The New Yorker*. It has been a publicly held company but now it will be privately owned, Newhouse having acquired all the stock for too great a price—$200 per share. At a meeting of stockholders, across the street from the magazine's offices at 28 West 44th Street, the acquisition is made official. When the meeting is over, I cross the street and, as it happens, get into an elevator just before Newhouse himself does. I press the button for the twentieth floor.

Newhouse is smiling gladsomely. "Do you work for *The New Yorker*?" he says.

"Yes, I do."

"May I ask your name?"

"Dan Menaker."

"I'm Si Newhouse," he says.

"Yes, I know. I was just at the meeting. I am—I was a stockholder in a very minor way. Congratulations."

"Thank you. Are you an editor?"

"Yes."

"Do you work with fiction or nonfiction?"

"Mainly fiction."

"Great! I can't wait to sink my teeth into that Alice Munro story we're publishing next week."

Newhouse has promised to keep the offices of *The New Yorker* physically separate—in a different building—from the offices of Condé Nast, which he also owns. He has promised to keep William Shawn on as Editor for as long as he wishes to remain. He has promised to consult with the staff when and if a new Editor needs to be appointed.

He doesn't keep any of those promises.

Forty-six

My father, eighty-three, senile but otherwise pretty functional, has a cardiac problem that has him in Nyack Hospital. My mother and I consider putting him into a nursing home after he's released. But he dies of a ruptured aortal aneurysm in the hospital at night, alone. A nurse tells us he said he was very cold, and she gave him an extra blanket and returned a few minutes later to find him dead.

Even in his method of dying, my father relegates himself to a kind of second-class family citizenship, or to being my mother's third child. Or maybe he was her first. He slept in a small separate bedroom in the house in Nyack—ostensibly because of his loud snoring. Whenever my brother or I accomplished anything notable, or my mother was promoted or in some other way recognized, my father would be pleased but would almost always add, "It makes me feel inadequate." But he was my father, and in his way a charming and debonair man, and intelligent. But he was also the youngest of seven, and a replacement child at that, as another boy before him had died in infancy, and he never seemed to get out of the shadow of his more enterprising family and then of his redoubtable wife. The love I feel for him after he's gone contains more than one kind of sadness.

Forty-seven

I publish a second book of stories called *The Old Left*. It's better received than the first one was, as any grocery list would have been.

An acquaintance at a party says to me, "Hey, Dan! I saw your little book in a store — I forget which one."

"Which book or which store?"

"Both."

Fifty-one

Robert Gottlieb, the former Publisher of Knopf, has been Editor of *The New Yorker* for about five years.

Let me back up a little here. After Shawn put off his departure as long as he could, Newhouse finally required him to name a date. I guess he did. Meanwhile, it seems that Gottlieb and Newhouse had been huddling about Gottlieb's eventual succession to the position. When Newhouse formally announced Gottlieb's appointment, a huge staff meeting took place at *The New Yorker*'s offices, at which Lillian Ross and others led the protest against this act of *lèse gotrocks*. A letter asking Gottlieb not to accept the position was drafted and sent to him. Scores of writers and editorial employees signed it. I was one of them. I signed out of naïve outrage over Newhouse's breaking his promise to consult with the magazine's staff before making this choice. It was all pretty silly. Many who signed the letter wrote privately to Gottlieb explaining that their objections were based on principle, not on his character or qualifications. The private letters were also, obviously, based — maybe even based primarily — on the signatories' hope to keep their jobs. Mine certainly was.

In any case, these five years have been wonderful years for me. They will turn out to be perhaps the best professional period of my life, thanks to Gottlieb's eclectic taste in fiction and his willingness to take chances with new writers. Few people will later understand what Gottlieb achieves for the magazine through his endorsement of more adventuresome and surprising short fiction. It proves to be his signal achievement, one that will turn out to have a significant and enduring effect on the literary world from that point on. A large part of an entire generation of important American writers finds its first prominence in the magazine's pages.

Forward again, five years. I am up in the country, on a weekend in June, in what I still think of as Enge's house, with my wife and our two children, William, eight years old, and Elizabeth, five.

The phone rings. It's my friend and former Fiction Department colleague Chip McGrath, moved up to Deputy Editor of *The New Yorker* under Gottlieb. Chip says, "Newhouse has fired Bob and appointed Tina Brown." Tina Brown has been running *Vanity Fair* for some years and has evidently worked her way into Newhouse's favor.

"You called that one," I say. (Whenever I complained about Gottlieb, Chip would say, "Be grateful it isn't a lot worse. It's probably going to be.") "When is she arriving?"

He tells me.

I say, "You and I will be gone in two years."

Shortly after Tina Brown arrives at *The New Yorker*, she takes me to lunch in a newly renovated hotel, the Royalton, with its newly renovated restaurant, very moderne in a random and pointless way: rhinoceros-horn-shaped lights in the lounge, a men's room with an eternally flushing water wall, and sinks that look like salad bowls. The restaurant is called 44, because the hotel's address is Whatever West 44th Street, about a block north of *The New Yorker*. Still, as usual, and despite this proximity and despite Tina's having become a habitué of the place, the route confounds her and I have to be her guide. "We turn left here, Tina."

"What should I do, Dan?" she asks me after we sit down. It's a little closer to "Dahn." "Tell me about the Fiction Department. What do you think—how should it work?"

I can remember only one detail of the conversation that followed, no doubt because I had very little new or enlightening to say, the old and unenlightening no doubt being: The quality and range of *The New Yorker*'s fiction distinguishes it from every other magazine in America. We receive more than two hundred unsolicited stories every week. I think the Editor of the whole magazine—namely, you—should continue to make the final decision about what stories to accept and publish. And so on. Oh, maybe I gave my opinion about some other editors. But the one specific moment I recall is what I said about Roger Angell: "It seems presumptuous of me to even talk about him this way, but Roger is just crucial to the history of this magazine—by family, by his own writing, by his work with fiction writers, by writing the Christmas Poem, and in many other ways. If I were you, I'd be very careful to preserve and even enhance his place at *The New Yorker*. He can be cranky sometimes, but his goodwill toward you is really essential, I think."

This conversation is a new experience for me. Unlike my friend Chip—a formerly Designated Successor, and Deputy Editor to Gottlieb and Brown—I have almost never been privy to any highest-level discussions about *The New Yorker*'s personnel, editorial direction (except in fiction), hiring, firing, art, "look," assignments, and so on. Not under Brown, not under Gottlieb, and certainly not under William Shawn. I mightily wish I had been. So as an insider I still feel like an outsider. (As I often do elsewhere in my life, after Mike's death.) This position affords me some perspective on what I do know about *The New Yorker*, but it also has excluded me from its innermost workings. So I am not "defending" Roger. Tina has asked me what I think she should do. I have told her. It would have been more than presumptuous—indeed absurd — for me to think that Roger could in any way depend on any kind of endorsement from me.

Some months later, Tina takes me to lunch at the new Royalton Hotel again, across 44th Street from the fabled Algonquin. "Dan, what do you think of Bill Buford?" She says "Booford." Buford is the Editor and one of the founders of the new version of *Granta*, a very good literary quarterly published in England.

"There goes my job," I say.

"Don't be ridiculous. I'm not going to hire him."

"Oh, you probably are. You may not know it yourself — I realize that."

"Well, you're a chippy sod."

"I think *Granta* is terrific," I say. I used to try to get Gottlieb to go after Redmond O'Hanlon, one of *Granta*'s best writers. "But from what I know of how it runs, or doesn't, I don't think Bill Buford would do well at a weekly magazine. I mean, it's a quarterly, but sometimes it manages only three issues a year."

Fifty-three

"Dan, Dan — what great fiction do we have on the bank?" Tina asked me near the start of her reign.

"There's a terrific long story by Alice Munro called 'The Albanian Virgin.'"

"Great! I'll read it this evening."

"Tina, did you read the Munro?" I asked her the next day.

"I mean, it's awfully long, isn't it? And it really does drag."

"Well, I don't think so. But we can just keep it for a while if you'd rather not make room for it now."

"Yes, let's wait and see. Let's look for something else for now."

• • •

"Fabbelis!" Tina is saying now. My Fiction Department assistant, Jay Fielden (who will go on to be Editor in Chief of *Men's Vogue* and other prominent magazines), and I have been presenting some of our ideas for *The New Yorker*'s first Fiction Issue (my idea, and for once not my mistake) to a group of editors. We're in Tina's huge, glistering-white office. Big windows face south over Bryant Park and the main branch of the New York Public Library. Jay and I had been looking through the archives there the previous week.

"And we found a lot of wonderful correspondence to and from William Maxwell," I say. "Notes, routing slips, edited galleys, letters from O'Hara, Cheever, Mavis Gallant. I thought maybe a tribute to Maxwell would be a good idea." I show copies of some of what we found. It looks good.

"Fantastic!" Tina says.

But there is a chill in the air. What is happening?

"Here's a great note to Updike," I say. I pass the slip of paper around. Roger Angell hands it along without looking at it. His face is set like a mask. Well, that's where the chill is coming from. But why?

"And do we have a good long story for the center of the issue?" Tina says.

"Well, I hesitate to mention it, but we have had that Alice Munro story on the bank for months now," I say.

"I *love* Alice Munro," Tina says.

"Well, maybe you could take another look at the story," I say.

She appears to have no idea what I'm talking about. "What's the title?" she says.

"'The Albanian Virgin,'" I say.

"I'll look at it tonight."

It is now psychologically as cold as a meat locker in her office. Has no one else noticed?

After the meeting, three or four of us are walking back toward the Fiction Department's offices, Roger stalking in the lead. He turns right at the end of the hall, walks a few steps into his big corner office, and slams the door like I've never heard a door slam before. The latch click sounds like an ignition switch followed instantly by the detonation of the whole door violently arrested by its frame.

I go into Jay's small office. "What is going *on?*" I say.

"I don't know," Jay says. "But he sure is steamed about something."

"Did you feel it in Tina's office?"

"Yes, but no one else seemed to."

I go into my own office, narrow but nice enough. Ten minutes later, I get up my nerve and go out and knock on Roger's door. "I think you're angry at me," I say when I go in and stand in front of his desk. "But I don't know why."

"I'm just furious, Dan." He is glaring down at his desk.

"But why? What did I do?"

"First of all, you didn't tell me anything about these ideas."

"Jay and I didn't tell anyone," I say. "We thought it would be a pleasant surprise. You know—fun."

"Never mind. Forget about it. Forget about it. Just leave me alone."

I am shaken and bewildered. Back in my office, after a few minutes, I begin to wonder what was second of all, and third.

The next day, I run into Tina in the hall. "Dan, Dan—I read 'The Albanian Virgin' last night," she says. "It's *astonishing!* Perfect for the main story in the issue."

Harold Evans, the Publisher of the Random House Publishing Group, a division of the Random House Corporation, calls me at *The New Yorker*. "I'd like to have a word with you," he says. "Can we have coffee sometime, perhaps?"

"What's this about?" I ask.

Evans and I have met at parties given by his wife, who happens to be Tina Brown. He once asked me if I played squash, and when I said yes, he found an old squash racquet of his and proudly showed it to me. "That's a real vintage item," I said. "Are you making a remark about my age?" he asked, brandishing the racquet at me. (At that same party he asked a friend of mine, "Did you read History at university?" and my friend, not knowing the British academic locution, said, "No—who's the author?")

On the phone Evans answers me: "You'll see. When can we meet?"

"How about today?" I figure he is going to ask me to co-write or ghost-write a book, or offer me a job. The second possibility doesn't fully register with me.

"Let me check with my assistant," Evans says. A minute or so later, he says, "Well, yes—can you come up right now?" The vowels, in his Beatles-esque Manchester accent, make the words sound a little like "coom oop."

At the elevator bank of *The New Yorker,* I run into Nancy Franklin, later to become the TV critic for the magazine. We have known each other and worked together for years. We call each other "Nosy," for "Nosy Parker"—the British slang term for a snoop. "Where are you going at this time of day, Nosy?" Nancy says.

"To see Harry Evans," I say.

"What about?"

"I don't know. Maybe he's going to offer me a book contract. Or a job."

"Oh, no!" she says. And it is at this point, with a version of that old cold, sick feeling, that I realize what's going on. It's my strong suspicion that Tina now actively wants me out of the magazine and has persuaded her husband to offer me a job.

• • •

"See here, I want you to come to Random House and lose some money for us with literary books," Harry says to me half an hour later. "I'll pay you considerably more than you earn at *The New Yorker*." He says "Random House" this way: "Random *House*," the way my friends from Philadelphia say "cottage *cheese*."

He goes on: "I know it will be hard to leave *The New Yorker*. I mean, you've been there for quite a while. Five or six years, is it?"

"Twenty-six," I say.

A cloud of embarrassment crosses his face. "But that can't be," he says. "You moost have started work there when you were fifteen."

"Twenty-seven," I say. "I'm fifty-three." To myself I say, "Nice save. Nice *try* at a save, anyway."

Another cloud scuds by, this one of not-quite-concealed consternation. What has his wife gotten him into?

The next day, I go to see Tina. I say to her, "As you certainly know, Harry has offered me a job."

"Yes, I know, Dan. Of course we'd hate to lose you," she says, far too quickly. "But I won't bar the door."

No kidding, I think.

"You see, Harry and I have this policy, if we want to hire someone who works for the other person," Tina continues. "We have to wait at least a year before ..." She goes on with an account of this spousal-professional pact meant to convince me of her husband's active quest to retain my services for Random House—to keep me from thinking she said to him the night before, "Harry, will you take this fellow Dan Menaker off my hands? He might work out, you know."

"Well, you could keep me if you wanted to," I say.

"I'm afraid we couldn't get close enough to the salary Random House is offering."

"You could make me officially head of the Fiction Department," I say. "I do all that work anyway—watch the bank, do the nominations for awards, watch the slush pile, do the scheduling."

"I wish I could but I can't. Roger would be too upset. He has complained to me about the situation down there from time to time."

"He has? What situation?"

"But the Random House job is a great opportunity," Tina says.

(You doubt my doubt about Harry Evans's yearning for me at Random House? A little paranoid, maybe? OK, well, a little while into my tenure at RH, Harry will ask me, through someone else, what I think of the idea of hiring another *New Yorker* editor— someone who I know is just not working out at the magazine. For the first and last time in my life, I threaten to quit a job. For one thing, in my opinion, the person in question would not make a good book editor. More important, I'm afraid the hire would substantiate in the eyes of those few who watch such matters the suspicion that Tina was using Random House as a sort of small recycling facility for her own refuse. Me. The other person isn't hired.)

Only two people advise me not to take the job. Betsey Schmidt, who works as an assistant to Alice Quinn, the poetry editor, says I should stay. She bases this advice on the experience of her father, Benno Schmidt, who was Dean of the law school at Columbia when he accepted the Presidency of Yale. Betsey thought he shouldn't have made that move—that if he had remained at Columbia he might have been appointed to the Supreme Court. A bathetic comparison—him to me, I mean—if ever there was one.

The other skeptic is John Sterling, a publisher who has also been an agent and a writer. He tells me at lunch, "You do realize that what you will be doing is essentially a sales job. If seventy-five per cent of what you do now is editing and reading and writing opinions about fiction and twenty-five per cent is office stuff and meetings and so on, that percentage will be reversed."

The trouble is that despite the special Fiction Issue, Tina has cut the amount of fiction in *The New Yorker* by half, shunted it from the front of the magazine to the back, and has everyone, on the factual and fictional sides, politicking and meeting and competing for her favor and attention. Some editors hold finished pieces back from her so that when they think there may a chance for them to run, they will take on the stop-the-presses urgency that she loves, and seem fresh to her eye. Hot!

So I wouldn't be losing what I had under Gottlieb, which was a kind of heaven for me, out from under three thumbs—of Shawn and Roger and my friend Chip—and publishing, for the first time in the magazine and often anywhere, such writers as Cynthia Kadohata, Michael Chabon, Jennifer Egan, Michael Cunningham, Allegra Goodman, Amy Bloom, Antonya Nelson, Abraham Verghese, Elizabeth Jolley, Ann Cummins, George Saunders, Ann Packer, and Noah Baumbach. That's already gone.

So in the fall of 1994, I take the Random House job, but I want to start in January of 1995, so that I can finish a novel I'm working on, called *The Treatment,* an extension of four stories I've published in *The New Yorker.* Evans agrees.

(When I submitted the fourth of those stories, "Influenza"—which won an O. Henry Award, my second—to McGrath, he gave it to Tina to read. She gave it back to Chip, and Chip said, "It's the most sexually graphic story that will have ever been in the magazine." According to Chip, Tina replied merrily, "Yes, I know. My God! Dahn—call me for lunch!")

I've also said that I won't leave *The New Yorker* if I have to wait the full five years required to be eligible for all of Random House's benefit and pension plans. Because S. I. Newhouse owns both companies, Evans manages to have the job change classified a "transfer." So I remain fully vested, whatever that means.

When I formally accept the job, Evans says, "You have five years to fook oop."

Part IV

Isn't This Scientific?; The Sugar

Fifty-four

At the memorial gathering for my mother, my son, eleven—a would-be tough guy—dissolves into tears as people talk about her. My daughter, eight, leans forward in her chair and looks at her brother with surprise and fascination.

My mother made a practice of cultivating young friends. My girlfriends, Mike's wife, researchers at *Fortune*, neighbors in Nyack, nieces and nephews. In her last years, facing a solitary life in the big empty house, she and I arranged to have young students from the Nyack Missionary College board there for free in return for seeing to its upkeep, helping her with errands, and so on. All of these people stayed in touch, and many attend the service in her memory—which is for the most part fitting and moving. The last person to speak is Greg, my mother's last boarder. He does a bad job, unfortunately—choking back tears and speaking almost incoherently. It makes me angry.

But then I think how amused my mother would have been by this display, and that calms me down. And then I remember two incidents involving Greg that make my blood simmer all over again. Once, in the driveway at the Nyack house, Greg told me that he had been undecided about whether to take this course or that course at the college. "But I listened for God," he said, "and God told me what direction to follow. I heard His voice saying what I should do, and I felt so grateful." OK — that bugs me but really isn't so bad. Greg was lucky to have his traffic-cop God pointing him in the right direction. But then, as he is still gabbling and quasi-sobbing, I recall a conversation that my mother had with him shortly after being diagnosed with pancreatic cancer. She said: "I asked him, 'Greg, do you believe that when I die I will go to Hell because I haven't been born again?' And he got upset and looked around and sighed and knitted his brow, and then he said, 'Yes, Mary, I'm afraid that that is what God has decreed. You will go to Hell.'" When she told me that story, I said, "What the *fuck* kind of religion obliges its followers to tell someone with a terminal diagnosis, a very fine and moral person, that they are going to Hell?" My mother said, "That *she is* going to Hell.' 'Someone' is singular."

Later, I will recall how generous with his time and attention Greg had been to my mother, not only because of doctrine but also because of love.

"You want to buy this book, Dan?" my boss, Ann Godoff, says, referring to the first work I'm trying to acquire at Random House, a novella and shorts stories called *CivilWarLand in Bad Decline,* by George Saunders (just now lionized by the *New York Times Magazine* as I write this). I had edited Saunders at *The New Yorker.* (He was discovered in the slush pile by my assistant, David McCormick.)

"Yes."

"Well, do a P-and-L for it and we'll see."

"What's a P-and-L?"

"Profit-and-loss statement."

"____"

"You don't know how?"

"No. Sorry."

"I'll walk you through it. What's the advance?"

My only knowledge came from what I had been paid for my books, so I thought surely I should offer more. "Fifty thousand dollars?"

"For a book of *stories*? A lot of them have already been published. But OK, let's stick with that and see what happens. What's the payout?"

"Payout?"

"Start with how much of the advance the author will get on signing the contract."

"Thirty thousand dollars?"

"Twenty-five — half on signing."

"OK, twenty-five."

"On D-and-A?"

"D-and-A?"

"Delivery and acceptance."

"Well, twenty-five I guess."

"No — you have to have an on-pub payment."

"On-publication?"

"Yes."

"Twenty for D-and-A? And five on-pub?"

"Nothing for paperback on-pub?"

"Oh. Ten for D-and-A, ten for on-pub, and five for the paperback?"

"Nah — it's OK. You don't really need a paperback payment. But with bigger advances you do. I just wanted to mention it."

"Oh. OK. Fifteen and ten, then."

"OK. Initial print?"

"Initial print?"

"How many hardcovers are we going to print at the start?"

"Twenty thousand?"

"Too much. Ten."

"OK, ten."

"Second printing?"

"Five?"

"Good! Paperback printing, assuming we'll do it in paperback, which is open to question."

"Fifteen thousand?" A shot in the dusk if not entirely in the dark.

"Probably more like ten. Returns?"

"Returns?"

"How many unsold hardcovers will booksellers send back?"

"Five hundred? A thousand?"

"Nah. Usually figure one-third—in this case, five thousand."

"Whoa!"

"It's a shitty business, Dan."

"OK, five thousand returns."

"OK. Trim?"

"Trim?"

"How big is this book going to be?" She takes three books from the shelf in her office and shows me the three choices.

"The small one," I say.

"Right, an A trim. And the PPB?"

"PPB?"

"Plant, printing, and binding—how much it costs to manufacture each book."

"I have no idea."

"With this book—no photographs, short book, no colored or printed endpapers, nothing fancy—figure a dollar a book."

"A dollar a book!" I say.

"OK, what's the price?"

"The price?"

"What will a retail book buyer pay for this book?"

"Twenty-one ninety-five?" I say, using my own most recent book as a guide.

"Good. For now, anyway. The sales reps may want to price it under twenty dollars, though. So how much will we earn against this advance?"

"_____"

"Here's an easy way to approximate it. We make about three dollars for each hardcover sale, one dollar for each paperback. The agent probably won't let us have world rights, and there might not be any foreign publishers interested in this book anyway, so we can't include that in any estimation of revenues."

"So if we sell ten thousand hardcovers, that's thirty thousand dollars."

"Right."

"And say ten thousand paperbacks. That's forty thousand dollars."

"Right—so the P-and-L probably won't work. It has to show a profit in the bottom line. So we have to adjust the figures. Remember, you can't change the returns percentage."

"Increase the first printing to fifteen thousand and the second printing to seven thousand five hundred?"

"That ought to do it. Isn't this scientific?"

Considering that I was Harry's hire, Ann was being, and continues to be, remarkably generous to me in her tutelage.

Now I have been Senior Literary Editor at Random House for six months. I remain in many ways ignorant of the realities of book publishing, even though I've had two books of short stories of my own published, one of them, *The Old Left*, by one of Random House's sister divisions, Alfred A. Knopf. But it begins to dawn on me that if a company publishes a hundred original hardcover books a year, it publishes about two *per week*, on average. And given the limitations on budgets, personnel, and time, many of those books will receive a kind of "basic" publication. Every list — spring, summer, and fall — has its lead titles. Then there are three or four hopefuls trailing along just behind the books that the publisher is investing most heavily in. Then comes a field of also-rans, hoping for the surge of energy provided by an ecstatic front-page review in the *New York Times Book Review* or by being selected for Oprah's Book Club. Approximately four out of every five books published lose money. Or five out of six, or six out of seven. Estimates vary, depending on how gloomy the CFO is the day you ask him and what kinds of shell games are being played in Accounting.

Sometimes — often — a non-lead-title book's success emerges from pure randomness. I am told that it's always a good idea — and a tradition — to take a book to lunch with agents, writers, people in the media. So when I end up having lunch with a *Today* show producer, Terry Schaefer, I mechanically give her a copy of a first novel I've edited that Random House is about to publish, *Amy and Isabelle,* by Elizabeth Strout, about a high-school girl in Maine who has a sexual relationship with one of her teachers.

The producer actually reads it. She loves it. She gives it to someone else who works at the show. Strout is invited on for an interview. I watch the segment, and at the end the book's lovely jacket fills the screen for three or four seconds — very important, I'm told, though even in my ignorance I figured as much — and the book "works."

Most of my colleagues have told me that that jacket image isn't very good. After the book's success, editors and sales reps and publicity people start asking for the "*Amy and Isabelle* look" for novels with small-town settings and similar themes.

I sometimes think that many books at all houses are more nearly privished than published.

Fifty-five

As I go through my mother's and father's belongings in the house in Nyack, in the bottom drawer of an old secretary at which my father used to sit and pay the bills and curse, I find two pristine copies of *The New Yorker* of August 31, 1946 — the issue in which John Hersey's "Hiroshima" was published in its entirety. They are wrapped in what looks like shelf paper, a ribbon tied around them, with a note in my mother's small, tidy hand: *Save.* I'm sure she saved them simply because the writing was so good and so new, and the publication was so famous, and because, surprisingly, she had a sliver of the collector's set of mind.

Viz.: In the attic of the house, I find a brown box made of some kind of old-fashioned plastic, about two feet long, a foot wide, and eight or nine inches deep. It has a lid and a kind of belt that goes around it and is fastened on the top. I recognize it as the box in which I sent laundry home from college. My mother would wash my dirty clothes and fold them and send them back to me. "Believe it or not," I say to myself, as shame comes over me. I open the box. There, in a pretty large plastic food container, are the baseball cards I collected in the Forties and Fifties, often bought with stolen change. About two hundred of them. They are in excellent shape. A Mickey Mantle rookie card. Don Newcombe, Allie Reynolds, Gil Hodges, Jim Piersall, Warren Spahn.

When my mother was ill, I didn't visit her often enough. What would have been often enough? I'm not sure, but it would have been more often. Once, when she was in a drugged sleep on the couch where, home from college, I used to watch *Soupy Sales,* I was so impatient for the next nurse to arrive that I went out and stood at the bottom of the driveway and paced back and forth, muttering, like a New Yorker. I had to get back to the city for work, I had to get back for the kids, I had to get back so that I wouldn't be here. I returned to the house to find my mother awake, her eyes filled with fear. "Oh," she said, "you're still here." She relaxed a little. "I'm still here," she said.

A couple of weeks later, she was unconscious and her breathing was labored. But the hospice nurse assured me that she would hang on for two or three more days. So I called my cousin Janet Bingham, who had been driving over from Westchester County and sitting with my mother during this vigil period. I told her what the nurse had said and let her know that I was driving to the city to have dinner with my family. When I arrived at our apartment, on West 83rd Street, my wife told me that the nurse had called. I called back. My mother had died. To my surprise, Janet got on the phone. "I drove over, Danny—just in case—and I was here with Mamie when she died," she said. "But don't worry. I think she was just waiting for you to leave before she could go."

This turn of events at first made me angry—I saw my cousin's behavior as a kind of sneaky recrimination for my having left, and a kind of familial coup d'état. It took a few days for me to recognize the anger for the eversion of guilt that it was.

Enge died five years ago, leaving me his house and land in the Berkshires, and also leaving me with another, but smaller, sense of guilt, for not having attended *him* closely enough as the end approached. My excuses were that my kids were very young, my new job at Random House bewildering and demanding, and the three-hour drive up to Massachusetts and back usually required an overnight stay. But I did go to see him as much as I could, tried a nursing home for him—it didn't work—then arranged round-the-clock care for him at his house, called him regularly, managed his finances, and so on. And continued to learn from him—in this case, to try not to be alone in old age.

Enge's lover, Tom Waddell, the Olympian, had left years earlier, to live in San Francisco, found the Gay Olympics, take up with a new and younger man. He did stay in touch, loyally, and visit, but he was far away. Enge's friends in New York and Great Barrington began to fall away, because of death, inertia, the debilities of age, or defection from a man whose own advanced years were transforming his wit and mischievous charisma into often bitter criticism and complaint.

But when the house came to us, we did what we could to preserve its handsome look and at the same time rescue it from decrepitude, all the while wondering, "What would Enge say?" (When visiting the old friends who had bought his Guest Camp's land down by the lake and built a house there, Enge walked in the door for the first time, looked at the spiffy, modern place, and said, "Aren't you ashamed of yourselves?")

In any case, my family and I settle into the house—but we'll always feel Enge's eyes on us—and into the community where my last name still means something to local tradesmen and shopkeepers. My two uncles' camps provided work and income to the town. We get to know the place and the people.

And in one case re-acquaint ourselves with another link to the past. Pauline Kael has a house in Great Barrington, about six miles from Enge's—I mean, ours. She and I have become friends up here, now that we have both left *The New Yorker*. I'm visiting her at her house, on the hill above the town, one afternoon, sitting on the wide front porch. She has read a piece I wrote for the *New York Times Magazine* about Emmylou Harris and gives me a compliment about it. I tell her that once I'd been interviewing the singer, years earlier, backstage at Carnegie Hall after a concert, when we were both in our early thirties. She was in what seemed like a rivalry, a friendly one, with Linda Ronstadt. I'd fancied myself in love with Emmylou Harris, which distinguished me from perhaps four blind, deaf males in America. She turned away to say something to someone else, turned back to me, and said, "I'm sorry, Dave, what was the question?" I said, "It's Dan, but that's OK, Linda." She laughed. Ten minutes later, after circulating in the room, she came back to me and said, "We're going out to have some dinner. Would you like to come?" I said that I couldn't, even though I absolutely could — because I was just plain terrified. So the point was I absolutely couldn't. Oh, oh, my mistake.

Pauline listens. When I finish, she says, "You asshole!"

I laugh and say, "Thanks, Pauline — thanks for your understanding after I told you this mortifying youthful tale."

"You have to understand," she says. "I said that because when I was in San Francisco, at KPFA, Duke Ellington propositioned me. I was a young, swooning girl, but I said no too."

"I'm not sure 'propositioned' is the right —"

"'Asshole' is."

I'm being wheeled out of the operating room after hernia-repair surgery. The surgeon says that as I was coming out of anesthesia I was trying to tell a joke. "Something about a little piano player in a bar," he says.

"I know what it must have been," I say groggily. "Do you want to hear it?"

The surgeon seems uninterested, but I tell it anyway:

Guy walks into a bar looking sad and blue. There's another sad-and-blue guy already sitting at the bar. In front of him, and actually on the bar, is a miniature piano player, playing a miniature piano — playing it beautifully.

"Why do you look so down?" the guy sitting down says.

"I saw a genie yesterday and he said I had one wish, and I wished for a million bucks and I got a million *ducks*. But how about you? Is that little piano player yours?"

"Yes," the other guy says.

"But he's amazing—I mean, he's really good. You could really make a fortune with him. So why so dejected?"

"It must have been the same genie, a couple of days ago, and he said I had one wish, and do you think I asked for a nine-inch pianist?"

The surgeon smiles wanly. Then he says, with some excitement, "We can do that."

"What?"

"I mean, you know—we can actually *do* that, if you want."

"Are you saying you think I need it?" I say.

Fifty-six

I am trying to acquire two novels, one completed and the second under way, by a British writer. Ann Godoff likes the finished book, or takes my word for it that it's good, or she is in a good mood, and has authorized me to offer $100,000 for each book. On the phone to the agent in England, I say, with no guile, "We're offering a hundred thousand dollars for both books." He says, with acceptance detectable in his voice, "You mean fifty thousand for each?"

I hesitate, but not too long. "Yes."

"Done and done."

Roger Angell has taken me to lunch at a small club called the Coffee House. You aren't allowed to talk about work there. We soldier through the conversation, greet others whom Roger knows. On the way back to the offices of *The New Yorker*, a passer-by who hasn't quite passed us by yet steps in front of us and says to Roger, "Aren't you Roger Angell?"

"Yes," Roger answers, with some wariness.

"I just want to say that I think you are the best sportswriter in America," the guy says.

"Thank you." Roger smiles, warming up.

"No, I mean, you are one of the best *writers* in America. Period."

"Well, thank you," Roger says.

The two shake hands and we continue on our way. About thirty seconds later, Roger turns to me and chuckles and says, "That's what it's all about, Dan."

"What?" I say.

"Love from strangers."

Fifty-seven

Steven Pinker is in my office at Random House. I am trying to get him to consider writing a short, essayistic book in popular language on the question of free will. It has preoccupied me since college days, when I read about it in Introduction to Philosophy and then, more extensively, in an Honors seminar. And also, as I looked back on choices I (and others I knew) had made about life and work, I began to think that these choices were not really choices, as we commonly think of them, but simply what we were going to do, under the illusion of conscious decision-making.

One small but signal incident in particular has stayed in my mind. Ten or twelve years earlier, I was playing the outfield in a *New Yorker* softball game in Central Park. A fly ball came in my direction but over my head. I began to run back for it and then decided not to try to catch it—it suddenly didn't seem worth it. I just chased it down and threw it back to the infield. As I stood there watching runs score, it occurred to me that my brain and body "knew" that I couldn't catch that ball (I would have been able to, in my thirties), and *they* "decided" not to try. But my mind gave me the illusion that it, my consciousness, had made that choice.

So I say to Pinker, as we look out the window, "Do you think the people down there have what they think they have—free will, the way it's commonly understood?"

"No," he says. "But there are the *qualia!*" That is, the conscious perceptions that some nonphysical aspect of ourselves, outside the workings of our bodies and brains, is able to control decision-making. Given the fly-ball experience, and many other, far more monumental, and too often regrettable, decisions I have made—some of them deeply hurting not only me but, even more seriously, others—I realize, standing there, that I have been looking for a way to in some measure absolve myself of culpability for those actions. Not responsibility—I accept that; society, family, and individuals demand that we respond to the consequences of our actions that appear to have been taken freely—but *culpability.* That in some very important way, we couldn't have done anything other than what we've done.

Pinker decides that he can't do this book, owing to contractual obligations to another publisher. He notices a book jacket on my desk, for a collection of poems by Katha Pollitt. The title, fittingly enough, is *The Mind-Body Problem.* Pinker says, "Oh! You know, my friend Rebecca Goldstein wrote a novel with this same title. I'd like it if you could change the title of this book."

"Well, you can't copyright a title," I say. "And wasn't that novel published some years ago?"

"Yes, but I would appreciate it if this title could be changed."

I tell myself that I choose to table this request, and I will end up leaving Random House before Pollitt's book comes out, and so that turns out to be that.

· · ·

I am assigned, at Random House, to work with Michael Eisner on his autobiographical book *Work in Progress*. I meet him a couple of times, and he is perfectly congenial. He tells me how foolish it was for anyone to call any movie anything like *The Lemon Sisters*—inviting, as it did, all kinds of review snidery. "On the other hand, we had a great success with a movie whose title had three words that each by itself should have spelled death at the box office," he adds.

"What was it?" I say.

"Dead. Poets. Society."

This conversation takes place at a screening of *Armageddon*, the Bruce Willis movie in which one of Hollywood's evidently endless supply of earth-threatening asteroids is, well, threatening the earth. Near the end of the movie, the Willis character, Harry Stamper, stays behind on the asteroid because, owing to various malfunctions, the nuclear weapon that will split the asteroid in half and send both halves harmlessly skirting the earth has to be detonated manually. Before this act of self-sacrifice, Stamper argues with ground control about the necessity to stay on the asteroid—they are glued to their screens and instruments and are ordering him to leave. "You don't understand," he says, or words to that effect. "This is *real*. I'm actually *here*. I know what has to be done."

When Eisner and I are talking, I mention how telling I found that scene, what it says, underneath the melodrama, about technology versus real experience—real, direct presence. He laughs and says, "I can assure you the people who made that movie had no such idea in mind."

Remembering Professor Beardsley's seminar and his coining of the term "intentional fallacy," I say, "It doesn't matter what they had in mind. It's there anyway."

Fifty-eight

I keep thinking about *Armageddon* (which, by the way, was the top grossing film of its year, outdrawing even *Saving Private Ryan*) and a whole slew of other 1990s movies that seemed to have as a theme the antagonism between technology and the real world. It's part of the theory that popular culture—even, or particularly, schlocky popular culture—expresses the anxieties and concerns of its era. This amateur sociology began in college when my friends and I would leave an art film—some completely static French talkathon—and someone would say, "You want to know what that movie was *really* about? It was about *trees*. Remember, Claude is planting a tree in his garden when he first meets Marie, and then later, she hides behind a tree when she's trying to get away from Marcel, and then Igor uses a fallen limb as a weapon when the three thugs, who are all wearing Toronto Maple Leafs jackets—*leafs*, get it?—try to beat him up, and at the end Claude is pushing Marie on a swing."

But the more I think about *Armageddon* and other movies of the time, the clearer it becomes that many films are, inadvertently or advertently, showing real concern about the possible dangers of technology. *The Truman Show, Pleasantville, True Lies, Total Recall, The Terminator,* and so on. (Arnold Schwarzenegger may have been the least likely existential hero imaginable, but his biggest movies always involved existential/technological threats.) *The Matrix* stands out as the ultimate expression of this techno-anxiety, with its premise that everything we do and see and hear is essentially false or at least unreal—part of a cosmic hoodwinking that only Keanu Reeves can end, in the existential equivalent of his ending the rogue city-bus rampage in *Speed*.

So I write a piece about this cluster of films for *Slate*, and as a result, and as usual in the world of minor cultural commentary, and as I fully expected, nothing happens. What could happen?

Nothing, except to me. It, and advancing age, get me back to thinking about such grand questions—the ones people generally encounter in college philosophy courses and then with relief, if not happily, leave behind. Is there something basically illusory about our lives? What are we doing here? Is there such a thing as free will? And why is there Something rather than Nothing?

The randomness and meaninglessness of my brother's death probably explain part of this restored, late-blooming curiosity and bafflement about the grand questions. The adoption of our children has probably added to it. *So* random. What if my wife and I had applied to the agency a year earlier, or a year later? What if my parents had procreative sex the night before I was conceived. I begin to see that a vast ocean of chance has washed us all ashore here, with illusions of greater meaning and purpose and control over our lives than we have.

In contrast to this airy philosophical wool-gathering are the thick and unpleasant realities of my work. I dislike selling myself and my ideas and the kind of honeyed nagging that publishing requires of its book editors, but I do it. Atul Gawande has been writing wonderful pieces about medicine for *The New Yorker*. I have gotten in touch with him about the possibility of Random House's publishing a collection of these essays in book form. His agent advises him not to do so, as collections of previously published nonfiction essays generally don't do well. And she wants him to write an original full-length book as his first venture into book publishing.

I don't agree. I remember Berton Roueché's *The Orange Man* and other collections of his *New Yorker* pieces—Gawande's are under the same heading, Annals of Medicine—which became bestsellers. I'm thinking that Gawande, who is not only a stellar writer but a star surgeon at Boston's Brigham and Women's Hospital, would fare even better with a collection of his pieces. But his agent and he resist my overtures.

I see the agent at a party. I press my suit once again, in person. Either because I'm so persuasive (unlikely) or because Gawande doesn't have the time to write an original work, they finally relent. The agent sends out a submission to a number of publishers. I figure I have the inside track if I can offer an advance competitive with others'.

In order to make that competitive offer for Gawande's book, I have to get Vintage, Random House's main paperback imprint, to chip in, and it offers a minor amount. Other publishers are offering more money. The level has ascended. I feel desperate and go to Ann Godoff and plead to be able to raise our offer without substantial help from Vintage. No dice.

On the morning of the closing, Gawande calls me because he wants to work with me but has heard from his agent that the acquisition will go to someone else, because of the disparity in offers. "I don't want this to happen," he says. I tell him that I am trying to get more money from Vintage (which I am, still futilely). Five minutes later, the agent calls and says, "I understand that Atul called you about the situation with his book."

"Yes, he did—his book which I have been encouraging him to do for a couple of years now, and which I don't want to lose. I've been trying to get more money for our advance all morning."

"Well, he didn't have the authority to call you," she says.

"That's funny—that word has the word 'author' in it," I say. "I should think he has the right to do anything he wants with his writing."

"It's too late. The deal with Picador is done."

Oh, publishing! Publishing is an often incredibly frustrating culture. And a negative one. If you are an acquiring editor and want to buy a project—let's say a nonfiction proposal for a book about the history of Sicily—some of your colleagues may support you, but others will say, "The proposal is too dry" or "Cletis Trebuchet did a book for Grendel Books five years ago about Sardinia and it sold, like, eight copies" or, airily, "I don't think many people want to read about little islands."

When the proposal for *Seabiscuit* first came up for discussion at an editorial meeting at Random House, some skeptic muttered, "Talk about beating a dead horse!" When the eventual major bestseller *Reading Lolita in Tehran* was first presented, I said, sarcastically, at least to myself if not out loud, "*Reading* What *in* Where?"

Three streams feed this broad river of negativity. Most trade books don't succeed financially. Three out of four fail to earn back their advances. Or four out of five, as I think I said somewhere back there, or six out of seven, depending on what source you consult. Some books that do show a profit show a profit so small that it only minimally darkens a company's red ink.

This circumstance in turn increases the usual business safety strategy of self-protective guardedness. You're more likely to be "right" if you express doubts about a proposal's or a manuscript's prospects than if you support it with enthusiasm. And finally, the inevitable competitiveness among acquisitions editors will incline them to cast a cold and sometimes larcenous eye on others' projects. The "team" metaphor fits the editorial departments of publishing even less well than it fits other competitive businesses.

The worst case of this competitiveness I have ever known about: A newly arrived colleague gets in a proposal for an autobiography by a leading political figure. The new colleague goes to lunch with a more seasoned and unprincipled senior person.

They discuss the new proposal. The veteran goes back to his office and calls the agent involved and says, "We've decided that I'll take the lead on the _____ autobiography." This is just treachery without guile, and nearly beyond belief. (When the situation comes to light, it is rectified.)

Those three acquisition-time negativities are only the beginning of the negativities that editors must face. Barnes & Noble doesn't like the title. The author's uncle Joe doesn't like the jacket. The writer doesn't like the page layout and design. The publisher tells you that the flap copy for a book about a serial killer is too "down." The hardcover doesn't sell well enough for the company to put out a paperback. The book has to wait a list or two to be published. *Publishers Weekly* hates the book. Another writer gets angry at you for asking for a jacket quote. (A famous author of legal thrillers began his reply to a blurb request from me with "If I even had to just answer all such queries as this from you and your ilk . . .") The *New York Times* isn't going to review the book. And so on.

If you work in the Editorial Department of a publisher, you usually don't know much about what goes on in Sales. That is, you can love a book you're working on, all your colleagues can — maybe uncharacteristically — share your admiration, your boss can talk the book up in marketing and sales meetings, but you don't know what sales reps say about that book when they make sales calls. I've always suspected that salespeople's and wholesale buyers' biases and preferences play a greater part in a book's fortunes than most editorial people want to allow themselves to understand. Reps and buyers are subject to their own "results" pressures, after all.

Further, genuine literary discernment is often a liability in editors. And it should be — at least when it is unaccompanied by a broader, more popular sensibility it should be. When you are trying to acquire books that hundreds of thousands of people will buy, read, and like, you have to have some of the eclectic and demotic taste of the reading public. I have a completely unfounded theory that there are a million very good—engaged, smart, enthusiastic—generalist readers in America. There are five hundred thousand extremely good such readers. There are two hundred and fifty thousand excellent readers. There are a hundred and twenty-five thousand alert, active, demanding, well-educated (sometimes self-well-educated), and thoughtful—that is, literarily superb—readers in America. More than half of those people will happen not to have the time or taste for the book you are publishing. So, if these numbers are anything remotely like plausible, good taste, no matter how refined it may be, will limit your success as an acquiring editor. It's not enough for you to be willing to publish *The Long Sad Summer of Our Hot Forsaken Love,* by Lachryma Duct, or *Nuke Iran, and I Mean Now!* by Generalissimo Macho Picchu. You have to actually *like* them, or somehow make yourself like them, or at least make yourself believe that you like them, in order to be able to see them through the publishing process.

To make matters worse, financial success in front-list publishing is very often random, but the media conglomerates that run most publishing houses act as if it were not. Yes, you may be able to count on a new novel by Surething Jones becoming a big bestseller. But the bestseller lists paint nothing remotely like the full financial picture of any publication. Because that picture's most important color of commerce is the size of the advance. The second most important color is the general level of book buying. I'd bet that the volume of sales of, say, the number 6 hardcover book on the *New York Times* fiction bestseller list in 2013 is, partly but not entirely owing to the advent of e-books, significantly lower than the volume of the number 6 bestseller five years ago. Four and three and two years ago, too, almost certainly.

It's my strong impression that most of the really profitable books for most publishers still come from the mid-list—"surprise" big hits bought with small or medium advances, such as that memoir by a self-described racial "mutt" of a junior senator from Chicago. Somehow, by luck or word of mouth, these books navigate around the rocks and reefs upon which most of their fleet—even sturdy vessels—founder. This is an old story but one that media giants have not yet heard, or at least not heeded, or so it seems.

Because let's say you publish a fluky blockbuster about rhinoviruses in Renaissance Italy, *The Da Vinci Cold*, one year. The corporation will see a spike in your profits and sort of autistically, or at least automatically, raise the profit goal for your division by some corporately predetermined amount for the following year. (The sequel to or second book after that blockbuster will usually command an advance so large as to dim a publisher's profit hopes for it.) This is close to clinically insane institutional behavior and breeds desperation rather than pride and confidence in the people who work for you.

Also, some 150,000 books are published in the United States every year. Let's—once again without any real foundation—be really draconian and say that only 10 per cent of those books would be in any way appealing to generalist readers of some intelligence. Let's take 50 per cent of that 10 per cent, for no reason at all, just to be even nastier, and we end up with 7,500 books. That means that on average 150 more or less worthwhile books are published *every week* in this country. Let's cut that number in half, just to make the floor of our metaphorical abattoir really bloody. That makes 75 worthwhile books a week. (By the way, that number is about twice the rough and generous estimate I've made based on actual experience.) How are 75 at-least-half-decent books going to receive serious and discriminating reviews in the few important places remaining for serious reviews every week? To say nothing of getting attention from prominent publicity outlets, like NPR and *Charlie Rose* and *The Daily Show with Jon Stewart*? They're not. They're simply not. These statistical circumstances make publishing into a kind of grand cultural roulette, in which your chances of winning any significant pot are very small.

More: The sheer book-length nature of books, combined with the seemingly inexorable reductions in editorial staffs and the number of submissions most editors receive, to say nothing of the welter of non-editorial tasks that most editors have to perform, including holding the hands of intensely self-absorbed and insecure writers, fielding frequently irate calls from agents, attending endless and ritualistic meetings, having one ceremonial lunch after another, supplementing publicity efforts, writing or revising catalogue copy, ditto flap copy, refereeing jacket-design disputes, and so on—all these conditions taken together make the job of a trade-book acquisitions editor these days extremely difficult. The shrift given to actual close and considered editing almost has to be short, and it's growing shorter—another evergreen publishing story but truer now than ever before. So you have to be prepared to give up reading for pleasure.

Still more: Many of the important decisions in publishing are made outside the author's and agent's specific knowledge. Let's say your house publishes a comparatively modest number of original hardcovers (and their corresponding e-books) every year—forty. Twelve on the etymologically amusing "spring" list, January through April; twelve in the summer; sixteen in the economically more active fall. Well, meetings are held to determine which of those books your company is going to emphasize— talk about most, spend the most money on, and so forth. These are the so-called lead titles for those seasons. Most of the time, the books for which the company has paid the highest advances will be the lead titles, regardless of their quality. In many cases, their quality is unknown at this planning stage anyway, because their manuscripts haven't been delivered or completely written or even begun yet. But why *should* the literary quality of writing figure heavily in this prioritizing? It's not as if the millions of readers being prayed for are necessarily looking for challenging and truly enlightening reading experiences.

I say "specific knowledge" because writers and agents surely have to realize that companies must practice this kind of emphasis triage. But they and you, as the editor, silently collude in trying to ignore the obvious when you tell them that the first printing of your book will be three thousand copies, that it will not have full-color bound galleys, that no advertising or tour is planned, and that it has been assigned to a publicist who up until yesterday worked in the Xerox department.

Why the collusion? Because this is a business fueled largely by writers' need for attention, and no one wants to crush a writer's dreams before a book is published. Especially because every now and then those dreams actually come true.

Speaking of the need for attention, if this hasn't become clear by now, an editor must be prepared to suffer transference from his writers as much as any therapist must from his patients. Many writers, like anyone else who performs for the public and desires wide recognition, no matter how successful they become, have an unslakable thirst for attention and approval—in my opinion (and in my own case) usually left over from some early-childhood deficit or perception of deficit in the attention-and-approval department. You frequently find yourself serving as an emotional valet to the people you work with.

All business and cultural successes spawn retroactive specious credit-taking. But because front-list publishing outcomes are so unpredictable, the false retroactive credit-taking in this enterprise can achieve a farcical dimension, as it no doubt does in the other media, especially TV and movies. Sales departments will claim credit for dark-horse bestsellers that they miserably undersold when they made their initial sales calls. A publisher who didn't want to acquire a book will often gladly accept and even court admiration if the acquisitions editor somehow overcame his or her resistance and the book was acquired and then became successful. Publicity departments that didn't bother to pitch a book with any conviction will run to get on board when the train picks up speed, and then say, out of breath though they may be, that they were on board all along.

One of the first novels I published at Random House was *Primary Colors,* by Anonymous, a fictional account of a Presidential campaign from the viewpoint of a black campaign aide to a candidate with a Southern drawl and a history of womanizing. For legal reasons, everyone tried hard not to refer to it as a roman à clef. But there was a lawsuit anyway, brought by a librarian in Harlem who claimed that people would think she was the character who has a brief encounter with a Presidential candidate who of course bears not the slightest — not an iota of — resemblance to Bill Clinton. I was deposed for four days, partly because I had made the mistake of using the term "roman à clef" in the book's flap copy. Being coached for a deposition will teach you the difference between telling the truth and telling the helpful truth.

In any case, the suit dragged on, as suits will, but it was finally thrown out of court, perhaps partly because the litigant was young and black and the character was middle-aged and Jewish. The suit also ran into the difficulty that literary libel accusations and charges of invasion of privacy often run into: The aggrieved party says people will think the character is him- or herself but also says that he or she would *never* do anything like whatever scandalous thing the character does.

So anyway, many colleagues in the Sales and Editorial and Publicity Departments discouraged the writer—whose identity none of us knew—and his agent and me from using "Anonymous" as the byline. No author to tour. No author to be interviewed. No newspaper stories about the author. No readings. Etc.

In my would-be-blithe, greenhorn's way, I liked the idea of no author's name, because it reminded me of contemporary and historical texts whose authors used (or sometimes suffered) anonymity or pseudonymity. *Go Ask Alice, Beowulf,* the *I Ching,* Mark Twain, Nora Roberts, George Eliot, Lemony Snicket. Because of the author's and agent's and my insistence, "Anonymous" stuck and became one of the principal reasons for the book's success. Many of those who had vigorously opposed the idea contorted themselves afterward into having not only supported but urged the idea. In fact, in a filmed interview about the book, Harry Evans, who was then still the Publisher of Random House, said that he insisted that the author remain anonymous.

Evans had come back from lunch with a well-known agent named Kathy Robbins and walked straight into my office with a manila envelope in his hands. He asked me to read what was inside and tell him what I thought. I took it home and read it over the weekend. As I said in my note to Evans, it read "like wildfire," though the ending seemed awfully abrupt—incomplete. He asked me if I thought we should try to acquire it and what I thought about the anonymity of the author. I said yes, and I liked the idea of the anonymity. So I bought the book, for $250,000, but in my conversation with Kathy Robbins I said that the ending seemed just sort of cut off. She said, "It's only the first half! Didn't Harry tell you?"

Primary Colors became an immediate bestseller, partly on account of the publicity and speculation generated by the anonymity of the author. Walter Weintz, a fine and very intelligent man, now head of Workman Publishing, who was then Associate Publisher of Random House, came into my office shortly after the book's publication and said, "You do realize how rare this is, don't you? Most editors go through an entire career without something like this happening." I hadn't realized it, though I did know that this success hit the book and me as the proverbial lightning strike—powerfully, and at random. I kept wondering what if—as was possible at the time—Clinton hadn't run for reelection. And later, just after 9/11, I saw very good books, especially quiet but excellent novels, get pushed away from any chance of literary recognition by a catastrophe of real life. The reception of any cultural production more often hinges on real-world vicissitudes than most people understand.

For all the onerousness and corporate foolishness and credit larceny, an editor does learn a huge amount about the world, especially if he or she acquires and edits nonfiction. And despite their intense neediness, writers are often fascinating and stimulating company. And most important, despite publishing's plentiful empty rituals, every day brings with it highly varied tasks and challenges. Every single book is its own particular enterprise, every agent his or her own kettle of fish, every writer an education (sometimes in dysfunction), every book jacket a unique challenge. And occasionally what you do has real importance to the world.

Fifty-nine

Cathy Hemming, Publisher of HarperCollins, takes me to lunch and offers me a job as Executive Editor, at a salary significantly higher than my salary at Random House, where I have been working as a Senior Editor for five years. I tell Ann Godoff—who has replaced Harry Evans as Publisher—about the offer, partly in the faint hope that I can get a good raise from her and stay at Random House, partly resigned to leaving, because once you threaten to leave, you probably have to leave if you don't get what you're hoping for, as I was pretty sure I wouldn't.

"Who made the offer?" Ann says.

"Well, it doesn't really make any difference, does it?" I say. "It's a respectable competitor."

"We can't match that amount," she says. "But you don't really want to leave, do you?"

"Ann, I have one kid going to college and one kid who will be going in a few years."

"Well, I got you a bonus this year, don't forget."

"I know, and I appreciate it, but still, there's a real differential in this offer."

"And we gave you a bonus for *Primary Colors*."

"Well, no, actually, I never got a bonus for that."

"Really?"

"Really. I was so ignorant that I didn't know that I might have gotten a bonus for that. Should have gotten one, I would say now."

"I was sure you got a bonus. I'll have to look it up and see what happened."

"Anyway, I'd like to stay, all things being equal, but they're not. Equal."

"We just can't match that offer, Dan—it's too much."

"That doesn't leave me a lot of choice, I'm afraid."

"This is Random House, Dan. You know you don't want to leave. Come on, tell me who made the offer."

"I'm not supposed to."

"Oh, come on. You know I'm going to find out anyway."

"OK—HarperCollins."

"I *hate* what they do," Ann says.

"What? Publish books?"

My mistake, but the die was so vigorously cast at that point that it didn't make any difference.

Sixty

I work at HarperCollins for so little time—less than two years—that it ends up feeling more like a walkabout than any kind of era in my working life. But among other worthwhile moments during this brief period, I have the good fortune to inherit Scott Spencer—a superb writer whose novel, *Endless Love,* has sold more than a million copies—from an editor who has recently died. And I have the best boss I ever will have, Susan Weinberg, the Editor in Chief. Direct, honest, confident, and a good listener.

A conversation that I have at HarperCollins with an agent stands out for its typicality. I'm trying to acquire a "Best of the Year" paperback collection. The agent (and a good friend) wants to "move" the series from its old publisher because he thinks the old publisher didn't do enough to promote it. Here is our conversation:

ME: How many copies did it sell last year?
AGENT: Fifteen thousand.
ME: Fifteen thousand as in twelve thousand five hundred?
AGENT: Yeah, about that. Twelve thousand five hundred.
ME: Twelve thousand five hundred as in eleven?
AGENT: Twelve-five as in twelve.
ME: So it sold about eleven-five?
AGENT: Yeah.

This is the way in publishing, as I'm sure it is in most other industries that produce physical objects for sale. Rounding up is fun. Rounding down is reality. Announced first printings of, say, a hundred thousand hardcovers often shrivel to under fifty thousand. Publicity announcements of an author tour of twelve cities shrink to New York, Washington, and Boston, and only if the writer agrees to use Bolt buses for transportation. "Reviews" generally signifies a misty hope rather than a guarantee.

No such playing with numbers in a doctor's office. "You got the sugar, honey?" a nurse asks me during my annual physical checkup. She's holding a piece of blue litmus paper in her latex-gloved hand. I do have the sugar, it turns out. It's probably a late-blooming effect of my infancy's illness — which has left me on a permanent quest for carbohydrates and sweets — as no one in my family has ever had this problem and I have remained pretty slender.

This diabetes will involve medication only, not insulin, since I exercise so fanatically and keep my weight down. But it's the first of three serious medical problems I'll encounter in my sixties. Paradoxically, these problems cure me of my vestigial hypochondria. The second problem is Graves' disease, which, briefly, is when your thyroid gets overactive and must be nuked. A nurse dressed in hazmat clothes hands you a leaden goblet that looks like something out of *Game of Thrones* and gives you a single radioactive pill. She then clears out of the room immediately, and you are left with your own private Fukushima. Your thyroid eventually gives up the ghost, and you have to take Synthroid for the rest of your life. The third problem I list here under "Coming Attractions."

I go to see William Maxwell a few days before his death. He is lying in a hospital bed in his apartment. His family and friends are hovering in the living room and dining room, signing remembrance books, discussing the calligraphy and the exquisite paper. There is some discussion about whom Maxwell has wanted to see and whom he hasn't. He is impossibly thin and frail-look-ing, but he smiles and his eyes are warm. I go to sit in a chair, but he motions me over to sit on the side of his bed. "It's so lovely to see you," he says. "I've decided there's not much reason to stick around, now that Emmy's gone, and I'm doing my best never to take another bite of food."

I say, "I hope you'll change your mind about that," and then I can't say any more. Maxwell grips my arm with surprising firm-ness, as if to say, Hold on. "When my mother died and I was ten," he says, "a man came to the door ostensibly to pay his respects to my father. But my father suspected that the man came in secret triumph or glee about my mother's death. It may have had some-thing to do with a sexual secret. In any case, my father opened the door, saw who it was, and slammed it in the man's face so hard that the house shook. I had never seen him do anything like that before, and I never knew until that moment that anyone could be so direct and angry in polite circles. And I haven't forgotten it since."

I am wondering why he has told me this story now. Well, of course it bears on death—on a death that changed Maxwell's life forever and has appeared in a number of his novels in one form or another. It may bear on my brother's death. It bears on the ques-tion of whom one might and might not want to see at a moment of past or imminent sadness.

He smiles at me serenely. He is some guy, I'll tell you. In order to veer away from mute admiration and gratitude, and tears, I go in the other direction. "You know, when you left me at the maga-zine, it took about three years for me to stop feeling completely unwelcome."

He puts his hand on my arm again, and with that warm and loving smile says, "I knew you'd be all right."

• • •

My fourth father leaves me. If I am ever to be father to myself, it will be now.

Sixty-one

Gina Centrello, who has replaced Ann Godoff as Publisher of Random House, calls me and asks me to return to the division as Editor in Chief, a position that Godoff held, in addition to being publisher. Centrello and I have lunch. It's my impression that since Godoff's departure some time ago, naming an editor in chief has become an urgent matter. I know, through publishing's chronic gossip affliction, that Centrello has offered the job to one or two others, who turned the offer down.

I don't. I do a little bargaining and we reach an agreement. I leave HarperCollins on good terms.

When I enter the Random House building once again, and then the conference room for the Random House division, I get warm applause from the forty or so people gathered there, most of them former colleagues. Finally! Something a little like the gang I tried and failed to organize at the Little Red School House, and like the "army" of kids at the Guest Camp who pretty quickly went AWOL.

Sixty-two

I run into Pete Seeger in the lobby of the apartment building where I live. He's going to visit the Weavers' producer of long ago, Harold Leventhal, who lives on the top floor. We get in the elevator together—he is with his wife, Toshi—and I say, "Mr. Seeger, my name is Dan Menaker and I've listened to your music all my life, and I just wanted to thank you for it." He says, "Why, that's very kind and you're certainly welcome. Now wait a minute—

'Menaker,' you say? Are you any relation to Enge Menaker, the square-dance caller many years ago?"

Maybe Enge is listening to this final rectification in his Marxist Heaven, where there proceeds from each angel according to his ability and to each according to his need. Maybe he and Readie will soon be arguing with each other over who should do the celestial laundry.

Sixty-three

Because I come to know that Diane Sawyer, the ABC newsperson, likes poetry, and I publish some poets at Random House—Billy Collins, Virginia Hamilton Adair, Deborah Garrison—we find ourselves in touch. I ask her to lunch, hoping to get her to agree to write a book. I offer her five million dollars, without any prior approval. She laughs and says, "So you want me to write about who Richard Nixon slept with." (She worked in the Nixon White House.) I say, "You bet." She says she can't write a book at this time because, as she puts it, "ABC owns my face"—a very modern kind of sentence, it occurs to me. She gets up after a cordial twenty minutes, and I finish the lunch with her producer.

People do read serious and worthwhile books. They don't have to be professors or editors or reviewers or the husbands or wives of people like that, or students or researchers. It's interesting to talk to Sawyer about Virginia Hamilton Adair, the blind poet who has published her first, very good book, *Ants on the Melon,* in her eighties. Sawyer is transformed from star to fan instantly, with no huge erudition but with a good reader's intuitive grasp of the meaning and feeling of what she has read. As a publisher and editor, you can sometimes forget that intelligent and sensitive people in all places and occupations and personal situations make books part of their lives. Not most of their lives, as you may do, but an important part of them.

Will Murphy, a colleague of mine at Random House, and I are meeting with Nassim Nicholas Taleb, the fierce Lebanese-born author of a cult philosophical/financial book called *Fooled by Randomness*. He wants to publish another, to be called *The Black Swan*, about the impact of "outliers"—powerful but unpredictable events—on our lives, and our tendency to fail to see events as randomnesses in favor of our brain's preference for retroactive narrativization and future forecasting. That is, we are evolutionarily programmed to try to make "sense" of past events, so that we can anticipate the future. When to plant the beans for the best harvest, etc. This programming does make sense until we try to apply it to highly complicated past and future occurrences that depend in large measure on happenstance and that proliferate as technology and the information it produces grow ever more complicated. That's what Taleb's book is going to be about, and given my preoccupation with such matters, I want to acquire it.

Will and I meet with Taleb at his hedge-fund office, or whatever it is, where his employees—I am guessing they are his employees—are constantly consummating their marriages to their computers. Taleb is an intense, black-bearded firebrand of certainty—about uncertainty, and many other topics. He rambles on, fascinatingly, about his book and his ideas, and parenthetically says, "I am of course an epiphenomenalist about consciousness. Sorry, it's probably not a term you are familiar with."

"I'm one too," I say. (I am.)

Taleb asks me to explain—to prove my claim—and essentially I do, thanks once again to that deep Swarthmore education.

He looks at me differently—that is to say, looks at me—and

says he wants to meet my boss right away. So we go back across town to Random House and hastily convene a larger meeting. Gina Centrello, my boss, skeptical of this philosophical zealot, says, "What happened to you in the big crash in 1987?"

"That is when I could have retired," Taleb says. Centrello smiles and looks at Taleb differently.

We acquire the book.

Sixty-four

Manuscripts and proposals and file folders cover the floor of my office. When Chip McGrath or David McCormick complains about the work he has to do, I always say, "I wish you could sit in my chair for ten minutes if you want to know what real hard work is like." Or it seems that I always say that, because one day when I'm having dinner with Chip after we see a junky movie, as we do once a month or so, he says, "I wish you could sit my chair for ten or fifteen minutes, and then you'd know what real hard work is." Then he laughs, and I realize he's mimicking me, though I hadn't been aware of the frequency of my resort to this rhetoric. (One day at lunch, I say to McCormick, "That's a good idea," and he says, "It is and it isn't," and laughs the same way Chip laughed about sitting in my chair. I realize for the first time that I use this equivocal device very often. Well, I do and I don't.)

But the work *is* hard. In fact, I think it's impossible to do an Editor in Chief's job very well—or at least fully conscientiously—for any length of time, and at that only a little harder than doing the job of a non-executive acquiring editor, especially in publishing as it stands—maybe I should say stumbles—right now. Electronic-book sales have begun in earnest, making acquisition and prediction of success, to say nothing of the idea of copyright, all the more complex, if not chaotic. Add that to the traditional and tectonically opposing demands on publishing—that it simultaneously make money and serve the cause of literature—and you have a fine stew of what corporations and politicians call "challenges." I call it a mess.

If I belong anywhere, it probably isn't in publishing. But, then, I felt I didn't belong in academia, or, at the beginning and near the end, at *The New Yorker*. Or grading high-school essays. I keep forgetting that this sense of dissatisfaction explains why work is called "work." I keep forgetting the good insights I gained from psychoanalysis and from simple but hard reflection—that my problems with authority are as much problems with myself as they are problems with authority, that like the teenager I was and in some ways still am, I grouse about and make fun of what I have to do and the people who tell me I have to do it, even when those people are me. For all kinds of reasons—illness, family imbalance, spoiling and its consequent narcissism, tragedy—I simply have not grown all the way up. Period. And never will.

But then again, I know very few people who have grown all the way up. The best most of us can do is manage intermittent maturity. For me it generally means forcing myself to take things seriously; this was especially important in the raising of my children and in my work as Editor in Chief.

The subject puts me in mind of a friend's son who took group Yamaha piano lessons when he was seven, and who, at the end of every exercise, would tap out the little tune of "Shave and a haircut—two bits." This is the kind of ironic stunt it's always hard for me to resist.

A colleague at Random House asks me to go over a letter he has written—in response to a popular-science book proposal—in which he refers to an evolutionary biologist whom the proposal identifies as Dobzhinsky. I say, digging up a datum out of my recollection of Dr. Enders's excellent Introduction to Biology course at Swarthmore, "I think that should be 'Dobzhansky.'" My colleague goes to his office and looks it up and then comes back into my office and says, "How do you *know* this shit?"

I'm largely able to put aside my iconoclasm and irony. Or put them in the closet, anyway. The people who report to me seem to like and respect me. I don't think I've ever been on this side of group admiration before, for all those childhood efforts. At HarperCollins it was beginning, maybe as a long-term after-effect of analysis, or maybe it was just accrued experience. It amazes me now. It doesn't really seem to be *me* calming feuds, gently reprimanding, giving praise sincerely but also motivationally, managing not to be a wise guy to my boss. Being judicious. Not spray-painting my high-school-class numerals on the walls, not sending prank gay-Valentine's cards to my colleagues, as I once did to McGrath at *The New Yorker*. Not fomenting union drives. Not seeking acknowledgment for things done well but finding satisfaction in doing them well. It's as if I were playing a joke on my true self, but it's a serious joke, and it is becoming part of my true self.

The advice I give to others generally takes the form of a question, one that I finally am asking myself: Do you want justice— do you want to *show them*—or do you want to achieve your goal? The two sometimes—frequently—don't go together. I stop being angry, or, anyway, I plug up the deep well my anger so often spouts from. In business, for people who want to and have the skill to "get ahead," seeking justice in tough situations leads to failure time and time again.

It also seems to work to try to put myself in the psychological shoes of the person who comes to me with a complaint or a problem and to ask that person to see the problem from the point of view of whoever else is involved. A brilliant young man asks me for help getting a jacket image changed—for the eighteenth time, or something like that. I tell him I'm not sure I can help; the art department is under terrific pressure. We talk for a while and he leaves content to let the matter rest. He says, "I don't know why it is, but every time I come in here, even when you say no, I feel better."

All well and good, and a very nice compliment. The trouble is, the jacket should definitely be changed, and whatever I may have gained in maturity, I've lost in youthful idealism.

But this new control is not quite complete. Jonathan Karp, the Editor in Chief of Random House, leaves to run his own imprint, Twelve, at Hachette. As Executive Editor in Chief, I travel to Washington, D.C., to visit Laura Hillenbrand, author of the hugely successful *Seabiscuit*, to try to persuade her not to follow Karp but stay at Random House for her next book, and to offer myself as her editor.

There is a flag on her lawn. I say how I admire her patriotism, especially given who the President is at the moment. George W. Bush. We have a nice talk, and I leave with the certainty that she will remain a Random House author. When I get back to the office the next day, Gina Centrello comes into my office with an annoyed look on her face. "You said something negative about George Bush to Laura Hillenbrand," she says.

"Well, just barely," I say.

"You're lucky," Centrello says. "She's going to stay with us, but she doesn't want to work with you."

"Why not?"

"Because she's a good friend of Laura Bush."

Sixty-five

Recommended by a mutual friend, Siddhartha Mukherjee, a hematology oncologist at Columbia Presbyterian Hospital, in New York, comes to see me at Random House about a book project. He looks like a handsome young villain in a Bollywood movie. He tells me about the first written reference to cancer, in the third century B.C., in a papyrus attributed to the great Egyptian physician Imhotep, who refers to "bulging masses" in a person's breast. I get goosebumps. Premonitory goosebumps, perhaps. In any case, *this* is what makes publishing, even if only occasionally, so exciting. We talk about his idea for more than an hour, and I get extremely enthusiastic about it—it seems to me the perfect time for a grand book about cancer. I've always felt that if it weren't for making shaving cream in chemistry class in high school and being "taught" biology by Mr. Z., of the forsythia-homosexual incident—and my over-fond attachment to words, my mother's line of work—I would and could have been a doctor.

When I mention the project to Centrello, she expresses reservations about a book on cancer. But I want to acquire it anyway, and I do. It goes on to win the Pulitzer Prize, but from another publisher, because Mukherjee leaves Random House when, a year or so later, I do.

Speaking of leaving, shortly before Tina Brown leaves *The New Yorker*, Roger Angell invites me to lunch at the Century Association, a literary/artistic/business club on 43rd Street, across the street from *The New Yorker*'s offices. It's just a social conversation, just to see how things are going. But the morning before the lunch, there have been Tina Developments at the magazine, and it's clear after we sit down in the quiet, wood-paneled dining room of the club that Roger is distracted and more fidgety than he ordinarily is. After less than an hour, he begins to look at his watch. He doesn't seem to hear the question I ask him and doesn't respond to my attempts to engage him in something that might pass for real conversation. Finally I say, "Roger, it looks like you're really upset about what's happening at the office. Maybe we should just get together another day and you can go back and attend to what's going on." He says, "Yes, I'm sorry, Dan, but that would probably be a good idea." The social aspect of the lunch evaporates. Roger pushes back his chair, gets up, and says, "I apologize. But I like Tina and I'm worried about this situation. You know, I really care about her."

This surprises me. I wonder what kind of transferential mechanism is operating inside this estimable man of letters to make him "really care" about this smart but mercurial boss. Her mind darts this way and that, like a pond skater, relying on surface tension to keep her afloat.

Afloat. Tina and her husband, Harry Evans, have for some time now put me ever so slightly in mind of the duke and the king in *Huckleberry Finn*, floating down the Mississippi, affecting noble lineages, and fleecing townspeople right and left with their cons and impostures.

Tina came into the magazine talking about people and subjects that were "hot," wanting the "buzz," the "chatter." When somehow she and I got around to talking about this kind of thing, she said something like, "I know it all sounds awful, but we have to do something that will create *more* buzz, that will rise above all the chatter. I don't always like it myself, but we have to do it." So this was a chicken-and-egg problem, as she saw it, but as I see it now, she is the chicken and the egg.

For all this professional skepticism about her, on a personal level Tina has always impressed me with her intelligence and charm, and there is a warm vulnerability about her, beneath the glittery trappings and despite all the Brownian motion, that makes her hard to resist. So I guess Roger's concern about her does make sense after all. Also, a lot of my colleagues much later on will say that Tina's CERN-like smashing of some of the magazine's old-fashioned elements was a necessary step in its development. That *The New Yorker* needed the antithesis she represented to the theses of Shawn and to some extent Gottlieb, resulting finally in the magazine's current Editor, David Remnick, as a kind of successful synthesis. Maybe that application of the Dialectic does have some merit. Maybe. But I can think of three or four other people who I believe could have done the same thing with less chaos. One in particular.

Sixty-six

Speaking again of leaving, Centrello takes me to lunch and lets me know that she would like me to step aside as Editor in Chief. Why? Numbers, evidently. Prizes—lack thereof. My high salary. It comes back to me that Harry Evans, when he hired me, said, "You have five years to fook oop, and I have barely finished four years. Centrello and I go back and forth about what role I might play if I do step aside—a prospect that doesn't displease me as much as I would have expected it to, as you may understand if you look again at the age heading of this section and if you know that I was working ten to twelve hours a day and much of the weekends. Considering proposals, reading first novels, attending one meeting after another—art meetings, marketing meetings, acquisitions meetings, retreat meetings, advance meetings, meetings about meetings, meetings about canceling meetings—going to sales conferences, the London Book Fair, the Frankfurt Book Fair, and to lunches and lunches and lunches.

At one point, I offer to help Centrello find a replacement for the job. But soon, the Era of Good Feeling ends, and I finally understand that leaving altogether might well prove more beneficial for me than staying under the conditions that Centrello is proposing. The ultimate straw descends when Centrello offers me a position as Editor at Large with no office. *No office?* Her financial guy tells me that this has to do with tax considerations, full-time employment versus a contractual arrangement, but that's hard to believe. Centrello now seems to want me out, and I now want out. I'm out. What a shame that it has to end this way!

She shuns me—except for formal politesse in all those meetings—where once she had stopped by my office every day. During this "transition" (as they say in business, spackling over fissures in the corporate plaster), a reporter quotes me as saying that publishing-job changes, including mine, remind me of speed chess. My mistake. I say to Gina, "But speed chess can be brilliant." M.m. again.

Centrello is a good publisher. She does know the numbers. She has now stayed in this position longer, and with more success, than anyone else in recent history, including Godoff, Evans, Jason Epstein, Joni Evans, and other publishing luminaries. My numbers, insofar as they *are* mine, have been mediocre at best, though the group has had some great successes. I keep wondering if there are other, more personal factors at work, but in the end, in such situations, it doesn't matter, does it? When it comes to corporate life, especially at its higher altitudes, factors of all kinds tend to get tangled up with each other, and it's impossible to untangle them, and pointless, and fruitless, to try.

Prizes. Later, I will have to reconsider my agnosticism, as the numerous prizes "my" authors win may well be the work of an ironic deity. Elizabeth Strout wins the Pulitzer Prize for *Olive Kitteridge*, Colum McCann wins the National Book Award for *Let the Great World Spin*, and Mukherjee wins the Pulitzer in nonfiction for his book about cancer, and Reza Aslan, whom I brought to Random House, makes a huge hit with *Zealot: The Life and Times of Jesus of Nazareth*.

Part V

The Great Temporariness;
Crème Brûlée

≥

Sixty-six

Cancer. A white shadow, about two and a half centimeters in width, in the upper lobe of my left lung, shows up on my routine chest X-ray. My GP says, "This could be very serious," and tells me to consult with a pulmonologist. I do. The pulmonologist is a petite, confident woman. I ask her a few questions about herself, out of real curiosity but also to try to establish some kind of personal connection between us — a doctor strategy that I think usually results in closer medical attention. She mentions more than once that people have a hard time believing that she has children in their twenties.

She asks me if I ever smoked.

"Yes, from the age of twelve or so."

"A lot?"

"Never. Never more than half a pack a day, and usually more like four or five cigarettes."

"When did you quit?"

"Twenty-five years ago."

"Well, that means you have no greater statistical chance of developing lung cancer, if that's what this is, than someone who has never smoked."

"Do you believe that?" I ask.

She leans forward, as if about to impart a Mafia-grade secret, and says, "Statistically? Yes. Actually? No."

She asks me to come back the next week, after she has consulted with some colleagues.

I visit Readie in her nursing home on Fifth Avenue. She is in her mid-nineties now. She says, "Oh, Lord, Danny, where we lived when you were little was so different. Bleecker Street had all them little stores owned by the Italians. Once when I was wheeling Mike up there in his baby carriage, one of the men came out of that store where all the vegetables were, and he said to me, 'Hey! How come you iss-a so black and you baby iss-a so white?' Things has changed a lot since then, but still not enough. Maybe that black man will be President."

When she dies, Readie is buried in a vast cemetery out in Queens, next to her husband, Joe Rogowski, the veteran of the Second World War who met Readie when they were both working for Uncle Enge in the summertime. Her son, Raymond, asks me to speak about her at the graveside. Those attending the memorial are mainly black. I start to talk about Readie's loving nature, her care for me and my brother and Raymond, her good sense, her generosity, and I hear "That's right" and "Uh-huh!" and "Talk about it!" coming from those seated before me. And instead of just meeting Raymond's request as best I can, I get caught up and get outside myself and mean what I'm saying—there's no distance between me and my words. No hint of irony—that addiction.

The next appointment with the petite pulmonologist who has two sons in their twenties:

"Well, what do you want to do about this situation?"

"Get that thing out of there."

"Me too. When?"

"Now! I'll go over and lie naked on the street until they take me into the operating room."

"I would recommend one of two surgeons. One is fabulous but doesn't have such a great manner. The other is just as good and I would send my mother to him."

"I'll take Mom's."

My wife and I go to meet the surgeon. He tells me that they will put me under and biopsy the lesion and nearby lymph nodes, and if only the lesion is malignant, they'll take the whole lobe out laparoscopically, but if there's any spread, they'll sew me back up and give me chemotherapy and then do surgery.

Near the end of the consultation, in an effort to appear casual, I say to the surgeon, "Did anyone ever tell you that you look a lot like Jeff Daniels?" He smiles in a pained way and leaves the examination room. The resident who has been with us the whole time says, "He gets that all the time. He really doesn't like it."

Sixty-seven

"What surgery are you having today?" a nurse in what seems like a sort of pre-operative holding pen asks me before I'm wheeled into the operating room.

"An amputation," I say.

"What?" she asks. She looks worried.

"I'm kidding. A lobectomy of the upper lobe of my left lung." She laughs. "Right," she says.

"No, left," I say.

"Hah-hah," she says.

In the operating room, someone takes my pulse. It's something like 115. "What—are you nervous?" the surgeon asks.

"Of course," I say.

"There's nothing to worry about."

Yeah, right.

To start an IV, a young man who must be an intern jabs at my left wrist, which is laid out to my side, Jesus-on-the-Cross style. "No, look," a nurse says. She rotates my wrist, so as to make the vein stand out more, I am guessing, and that's the last thing I remember, except for the reverse golden-swastika hallucination that spins faster and faster as I go under.

I come out of the anesthesia in the recovery room at Mount Sinai Hospital after the surgery. For all I know, I might be waking up to find out that the surgery was not completed. My wife, Katherine, and a nurse are standing by the gurney. I am said to have said, "Did they do everything?" The answer was yes. I do remember a great flood of relief washing through me, as if my blood were resuming its normal, warm circulation instead of feeling like the cold soup it instantly became when I first saw the white shadow on the X-ray. I am said to have said next, "Did Obama win in South Carolina?"

A few weeks later, the pulmonologist, after managing to inform me again that people are amazed to learn she has kids in their twenties, says, "You have large lymph nodes, so Dr. Williams thought there probably was some spread of the cancer. That's why he wanted the biopsy." She leans forward confidentially and says, "I didn't think there was, and I am always right!"

After my recovery from surgery, I am at a big literary gala at the American Museum of Natural History, standing on the steps outside the museum, talking to Michael Cunningham, whose first *New Yorker* published story, "White Angel," I edited many years earlier. It caused a small literary sensation at the time—a time when short stories could cause literary sensations of any size at all. We are standing outside so that Cunningham can smoke. I've liked him ever since we worked together; he is warm and genial and gives the impression of happy self-indulgence. And even though he is ten years younger than I am, he always calls me "My boy!" when we meet. (Harry Evans always calls me "yoong mahn," but he is older, and for some reason it doesn't sit well with me.)

The Editor in Chief of a prominent publishing house is standing out there too, and smoking. She sidles up to us, and we greet each other. I introduce her to Cunningham, she goes on Alert Mode, and the next thing I know, I swear, I find myself physically elbowed out of the situation, with the EIC going at Cunningham like a terrier. It makes me glad to no longer have to be the tribal warlord that publishing and no doubt most businesses can turn you into. It also makes me concerned—as it always does after my operation—to see them both smoking. I'm tempted these days to go up to smokers on the street and beg them to stop.

Sixty-eight

A Good Talk: The Story and Skill of Conversation, by me, is published. It does OK, gets some good notices, and also gets me interview and speaking invitations. But it has an effect on others that I should have, but haven't, anticipated: It makes some people nervous about talking to me. And I do love to talk.

It's hunting season in the Berkshires. Our neighbor Ernie, who hunts our land in return for plowing the driveway and giving us some venison and bear sausage—a kind of barter descended from England's feudal days, I enjoy thinking, baronially—drives up the driveway to show us the huge slain black bear, more than four hundred pounds, in the back of his pickup. Its claws are as big and black as meat hooks, and even in death it looks dreadful. "If you eat the sausage," Ernie says, "make sure to cook it real good. You don't know what them bears have been eating—all kinds of garbage and dead things and stuff like that."

Having had surgery for lung cancer the previous spring, and looking at this magnificent animal brought down at random, I feel that the Great Temporariness has swung around from being a dark sidekick to a face-to-face superior who will no longer tolerate my disregard. Maybe he will wake up next spring with the huge black bears out there in the state forest, behind our land, and come hunting for me.

Sixty-nine

He does.

The pulmonologist with kids amazingly in their twenties finds three very small nodules in the remainder of my left lung on the annual follow-up CT scan a couple of years after my surgery. They were there even more tinily the previous year, but they could be ignored as inconsequential, but now, although they're still small, they're bigger. Or one of them is. Not good. She wants me to have one of them biopsied, by means of a needle through my back and the wall of my lung. I have it done. Malignant. Very not good. When the pulmonologist and I go over my options for treatment, and after I'm told that this appears to be an "indolent recurrence," and that it's perfectly possible that I will remain asymptomatic for a couple of years, I say, somewhat idly, "What if I decide to do nothing? Just sort of sit back and see what happens?"

The pulmonologist gets upset. "You can't do that!" she says. "That isn't an option. You have to be treated."

I say, "'I have been half in love with easeful Death.' Do you know that Keats poem?" She looks bewildered. I am the subject, I think, casting back to Professor Wasserman, and the nodules are the object.

I call Siddhartha Mukherjee, whose "biography" of cancer, *The Emperor of All Maladies*, I acquired at Random House. He recommends an oncologist at his hospital, and I go to see him about treatment. He is a wonderful man, funny, European in origin, Old World in his sensibility. I think he has read poetry at some point in his life. When I ask, "What if I decide to do nothing?" he smiles and says, "I hope you won't, but it wouldn't necessarily be so crazy."

He tells me to have a brain MRI, with contrast, to see if there is any spread to my brain, which is where lung cancer often spreads. (Puzzling.) Negative. He asks me to have a full-body PET scan, to see if there is evidence of metastasis anywhere else. Negative. The nodules in my lung barely show up.

For the brain scan, I have to change in a somewhat grimy bathroom, with paper towels on the floor, outside the actual MRI-machine room. The nurse is heavy and slovenly and comical.

MRI NURSE: OK, Daniel, you can change into the gown
      in the bathroom. ["Dahn-*yell*," she says.]

ME: In the bathroom?

NURSE: Yes, the bathroom—right there.

ME: The bathroom . . . OK.

NURSE (when I emerge): Oh, Papi, you look good in that.

ME: Thanks.

NURSE: I see that ring.

ME: Is it going to be a problem in the MRI machine?

NURSE: No. No problem, Papi. You have a wife, but do
      you have a girlfriend?

ME: Only if you want to be my girlfriend.

NURSE (to another nurse): Daniel wants to run away
    with me. Did you hear?

ME: I'll run away with both of you.

NURSE: You're too much, Daniel. Make a fist . . . Good
    veins.

ME: Thanks.

NURSE (snaps on a single sterile glove, flicks the hypo-
    dermic she's holding in the other hand): This is the
    contrast.

ME: Right. If you see something in my brain, don't tell me.

NURSE: I know what men are thinking about all the time.
    (Laughs uproariously)

ME: Not me — not under these particular circumstances,
    anyway.

NURSE: OK, *vámonos!*

ME: *Vamos a ver que pasa en mi cabeza. Espero que nada.*

NURSE: Oh, you speak Spanish.

ME: *Solamente un poco. Mi padre viajo frecuentamente en la
    América del Sur.*

NURSE: *Tienes que practicar, Papi.*

ME: *Claro.*

NURSE: Now I know we will run away.

In the middle of the subsequent five-session course of chemotherapy for recurrent lung cancer, at Sloan-Kettering, I write a piece
about the military language so often used in describing the treatment of the disease. The "war on cancer," "a valiant fight against
lymphoma," "new weapons in the fight against cancer," and so
on. I send it to an editor of the Sunday *Times*. She likes it, buys it,
and we agree that it can run anytime. All I ask is that it not run on
the Sunday before Labor Day, thinking that readership for a newspaper must be smaller than usual on that Sunday. And also mildly

congratulating myself for my sophistication about timing and publishing in general. So it runs the Sunday before that Labor Day Sunday—it runs on the day that Hurricane Irene hits and practically drowns the Northeast, obliterating anyone's interest in just about anything else.

I am in the country again, looking at our dog, Maxwell, in thirty-degree weather under tin-colored skies. The spring just will not come this year. He is *sleeping* in the driveway. Oh, to be a Tibetan, as he is—to say nothing of a terrier, and a cosseted one at that. He was digging a hole in the lawn for fifteen minutes, as industriously as a gravedigger, pausing to consider his work every minute or two, and sometimes going to the other side of the excavation site and attacking the earth from his own and more primal version of a different angle. It occurred to me that he was doing something like what I'm doing right now.

Maxwell is extremely curious. He will follow me around even after he has eaten, when he can't possibly harbor any hope or desire for more food. He wants to know what I'm up to, it seems. Everyone has had the experience of having a dog look at him with what seems like curiosity and the wish to be able to say something wise or important. Sometimes when I rub Maxwell's stomach—which he does not so much invite as suffer me to do, it looks like—he watches my face out of the corner of his eye, as if he were assessing my character. No wonder Mr. Maxwell kept his thinking dog in *So Long, See You Tomorrow*.

And once again, as my own mortality is pulling into the parking area on the lawn across the road from the house and, as my father did so many years ago, may soon be walking up the driveway toward where I have just now been playing with the dog, I wonder about that other story Mr. Maxwell, my fourth and final father, told me as he lay dying, the story about his own father's slamming the door in the face of the man who came to visit. The more I think about it, the stronger it grows in my mind as a distillation of Maxwell's character, at least as I saw it: the enduring influence of his parents; his spare, sure sense of narrative; his concern about decorum and its chronic destruction by love and hate; his capacity for blunt honesty; and the openness and trust of his friendship and guidance, which lasted through his final days.

I'm teaching a humor-writing course in Columbia's graduate creative-writing program. Through my agent, Esther Newberg, who is also Steve Martin's agent, I ask Martin if he would visit the class and talk to the students. He and I had a couple of near-misses in book publishing some years earlier. He was working on one of his books—maybe the novel *Shop Girl*—and was looking for a new editor, and we had lunch. He said, at the end of a pleasant but somewhat awkward conversation, "So, should I just sign up with you?"

"Well, I think you should definitely talk to other people." My mistake, bred of arrogance. Martin took my advice. He signed up with another publisher. But now, he kindly accepts my invitation.

I meet him at Broadway and 116th Street, at Columbia's famous gates. He's wearing a hat and sunglasses, and he dips his head down this way and that—the Celebrity Anti-Recognition Maneuver. I have told the students to call him "Mr. Martin." I add, "Don't ask for an autograph, please." The class goes well, but at the end, a couple of the students ask Martin to pose with them for cell-phone pictures.

Sometime later, inspired by Steve Martin's mastery of the banjo, I pick up my old steel-string guitar and try to play it and sing along. My fingertips have no calluses, and some of the knuckles on my chord-making left hand are arthritic—they look like pierogi. In the country, I try the nylon-string guitar that my uncle brought back from Mexico decades ago. It's a little easier on my hands but not easier enough to keep me going with guitar rehab. And I have no one to sing with. So instead I start prospecting around YouTube to hear the old singers and musicians I used to idolize: Ricky Skaggs, Emmylou, Doc Watson, the Greenbriar Boys, Earl Taylor and the Stoney Mountain Boys, J. E. Mainer.

After the biopsy, my YouTubing, especially as fueled by some excellent mediocre Chilean white wine, turns into making a list of songs I want played at my funeral: Liam Devally, an Irish tenor, singing the Gaelic anthem of misrule "An Poc ar Buile" ("The Mad Puck Goat"); Ricky Skaggs singing "Hallelujah, I'm Ready"; the Muppets' hilarious rendition of "Danny Boy"; and "Barroom Girls," performed with such penetrating melancholy by Gillian Welch and David Rawlings. Listening to this last, which puts me in mind of failed romances of long ago and of what my life has had and hasn't had—what I've won and what I've lost, what happened to my family, how little choice we all have about the choices we make, just the tears of things, the tears of all things—I find myself lost in tears. I think, tipsily, They'll miss me when I'm gone, though I know perfectly well that they won't, not most of them, not really, and certainly not for very long. The world, with all its impossible variegation and the basic miracle of its existence, draws most mourners out of their grief and back into itself. The homosexual forsythia blooms; the young Irish dancers in Killarney dance, their arms as rigid as shovel handles; secret deals are done involving weapons or office space or crude oil or used cars or drugs; new lovers, believing they will never really have to get up, lie down together; the Large Hadron Collider smashes the Higgs boson into view; snow drapes its white stoles on the bare limbs of winter; the crack of the bat swung by a hefty Dominican pulls a crowd to its feet in Boston; bricks for the new hospital in Phnom Penh are laid in true courses; the single-engine Cessna lands safely in an Ohio alfalfa field during a storm. How can you resist? The true loss is only to the dying, and even they won't feel it when the dying's done.

Seventy

When—despite the radical contingencies, the happenstances, that you know have determined so many aspects of your life, beginning with your very conception—you start trying to shore up its fragments into some kind of organization and meaning, your memory, despite its notorious unreliability, provides the most important information. It has already verified and falsified and winnowed the past in a way that begins to form, for you, patterns and through-lines. But though you have to distrust the memories that create these patterns, and though someone else might well see different patterns in them, in a way the ones you come up with can't be inaccurate. Because they are the patterns that *you* discern, and so they must be, in an important way, true of your life. Or at least say something important about it.

Still, if you have any conscientiousness and self-doubt, you will almost surely get up out of your chair and make an attempt to see if there's any research you can do to correct or reconfigure the narrative you've settled on. You can try to change or at least deepen your ideas about your life. This is the equivalent of the internal research—the rummaging around in dreams and recollections—that you do in psychoanalysis; if it is a good analysis, you come out not with a radically different view of yourself and others but with a more nuanced and less fantasy-distorted view.

The memory of Roger Angell cutting our lunch short and dashing back to the office to lend support to that odd boss reminds me of *The New Yorker*'s first Fiction Issue, and the research

Jay Fielden and I did for it in the New York Public Library, and Roger's angry response to the suggestion of devoting the centerfold to William Maxwell. I realize that somewhere in the dark corners of my mind I *knew* even at the time that the Maxwell suggestion would provoke Roger. My mistake.

But was it? It may have led to my departure from *The New Yorker,* ultimately, but I may have been seeking that very result without realizing it. And I was certainly declaring some version of final independence from Roger, a sort of complex father who had nevertheless taught me a great deal: how to be the host at a dinner party; how to write humor, and why co-writing literary humor doesn't work for very long; how to be firm with writers (in my own way); how to sound a note of congeniality in feature writing and in reporting; how to take a long look at events in the present that seem momentous at the moment but will prove not to be; how to keep the writing life in some semblance of perspective to the rest of life. Roger Angell showed me a more pragmatic approach to writing and editing than Maxwell did.

My need for an antagonist in authority (and a corresponding hero, William Maxwell) must stretch back in part to my family's reflexive demonization of those in power. We drew sustenance from being *against*. And from being for those who seemed of pure heart. One of the strongest recollections I have of my father is sitting with him and watching *Meet the Press* in its earliest days and listening to him mutter, "What a liar!" This reflex has given me not only a lot of trouble but also an incentive to persevere, to prove wrong those who I think or imagine doubt me.

The Library's *New Yorker* archives end in 1984 (with a little material going forward to 1988), so there's no Tina Brown dashing around in there, getting lost without anyone to tell her which way to turn to get to the Royalton. But I recall clearly the astonishment Jay and I experienced when we began to sift through those files. It was as though we were in Oklahoma in 1896 and had just struck oil. Here's what the archive's general description says at the start:

THE NEW YORK PUBLIC LIBRARY
HUMANITIES AND SOCIAL SCIENCES LIBRARY
MANUSCRIPTS AND ARCHIVES DIVISION
The New Yorker
Records
Compiled by Francine Tyler Library Technicians Sandra
Carpenter Sato Fleite Jeremy Megraw Gregory Poole
Alexander Thurman 1994
Text by
William Stingone 1996

SUMMARY
Main Entry: *The New Yorker* Records
Title: Records ca. 1924–1984
Size: 875.8 linear feet
Access: Two boxes, #1302–1303, labeled "Eccentrics, 1969–1975," are restricted until 2050; otherwise access is unrestricted.
Source: Gift of *The New Yorker*, 1991.
Historical Statement: *The New Yorker* magazine began publication on February 21, 1925.
Description: Included are general and editorial correspondence; editorial memoranda; holograph and edited non-fiction, fiction and verse manuscripts; critical notes on writings and ideas for articles; files, called "Copy and Source," containing materials to be published in each week's issue; reprint and permissions requests; letters to the editor; press releases and newsclippings; original art work called "spots" and tearsheets of thousands of cartoons; photographs, posters, and sound recordings.

Eight hundred and seventy-five linear feet! Two football fields, plus everything but the Red Zone of a third. (And don't I yearn to know what's in boxes 1302 and 1303, the "eccentrics" from 1969 through 1975!) So I decide to go back to the Library and look at some of the documents from the earlier part of my time, 1969 through 1984. Not so much because *The New Yorker* looms so balefully and dominatingly over my whole life, I hope, but because those years seem to me formative and transformative for my "career"—a word, you'll recall, that William Shawn hated, as he hated "gadget" and "balding"—and must contain some of the adjustments and correctives and enlightenments I'm hoping to gain from this project.

So down to the Library I go. The records are on the third floor of the imposing building, which happens to be on the verge of a major reconstruction, with many of its research resources to be stored elsewhere but supposedly available within twenty-four hours. A big controversy over that. Getting into the research room is more complicated than I remembered. You have to get buzzed in, as you would to a gold-buying store on the second floor of a building on West 47th Street, a few blocks north. You can't take any tote bags or briefcases or backpacks in there. For fear of purloining, it must be. Then you have to fill out a form, stating your purpose, your affiliation (university or publisher or whatever), and so on. The woman who hands me the form is wearing a turquoise sari and seems formidable. She looks at the tote bag I have inadvertently brought in with me and the guard outside must have missed. "You have to go back out," she says. "Those bags are not allowed." She is prim about this. Another woman in the small nest of desks and counters arranged in a square in the center of the research room says, "It's OK, sir. I'll just store it here in this cubby for you. You don't have to go back out again." The sari looks at the other woman with disapproval. I hand over the tote bag. The sari hands me the form, on a clipboard, and a pencil— one of those stubby things that they give you with your miniature-golf scorecard—and I take a ballpoint pen out of my shirt pocket and start filling the form out. The sari, who has looked away, and everyone else go about their business. I have some trouble getting the sari's attention after I've finished—ever since the Tote-Bag-Gate I have felt a little like Ralph Ellison in here—but when I do, and hand her the clipboard, she looks at it as if it were a stool sample and says, "It's supposed to be in pencil." I hand her back the pencil, as if it were a peace pipe, and she shakes her head sadly and gets ready to hand it back and give me another blank form. "It's OK," the tote-bag forgiver says—she must be the sari's supervisor. "You don't have to fill out another form."

Finally I sit down at one of the computers and a librarian gives me a brief briefing about how the archives are indexed, and I begin to troll and scroll through them. Their extensiveness is overwhelming. I begin to take some notes about the box numbers I'd like to see when the librarian comes back and says that I have to order the boxes I want to see and they will be found and made available in that room a day or two later. This is a relief. I have almost panicked while I looked at the Fiction Department correspondence index for a single year, 1976—my first year as an editor—and then beyond:

2 Adams, Alice
3 Allen, Woody 4 Ashbery, John 5 B–Baz 6 Banks, Russell 7 Barthelme, Donald 8 Baumbach, Jonathan
9 Be–Bez
10 Beattie, Ann 11 Berryman, John 12 Bi–Boz 13 Bishop, Elizabeth
14 Blount, Roy, Jr. 15 Borges, Jorge Luis 16 Boyle, T. Coraghessan
17 Br–Brz 18 Bradbury, Ray 19 Brickman, Marshall
FICTION CORRESPONDENCE, 1952–1980
371
A NEW YORKER RECORDS GUIDE
20 Brinnin, John Malcolm 21 Brodsky, Joseph 22 Bromell, Henry
23 Brown, Rosellen
24 Bu–Bz 25 Buechner, Frederick 26 Busch, Frederick
FICTION CORRESPONDENCE, 1952–1980
885 1 2 Cain, James M.

3 Calisher, Hortense 4 Carruth, Hayden 5 Casey, John 6 Ch–Clz
7 Cheever, John 8 Cheuse, Alan 9 Ciardi, John 10 Co–Coz
11 Coetzee, J. M. 12 Collins, Christopher 13 Colwin, Laurie
14 Conroy, Frank 15 Coover, Robert 16 Cotler, Gordon
17–18 Cu–Dez 19 De Andrade, Carlos Drummond 20 DeLillo,
Don 21 De Vries, Peter 22 Di–Dz 23 Dickey, James 24 Dillard,
R.H.W. 25 Diller, Phyllis 26 Disch, Thomas M. 27 Dixon,
Stephen 28 Domini, John 29 Dubus, Andre 30 Dufault, Peter Kane
31 Durrell, Lawrence
886 1 2 Eberhart, Richard
E 3 Elkin, Stanley
C-Caz
372

NEW YORKER RECORDS GUIDE

4 Ellis, H. F. 5–6 F 7 Friedman, Bruce Jay 8 Friel,
Brian 9 G–Giz 10 Gallant, Mavis 11 Garcia Marquez,
Gabriel 12 Gardner, John 13 Geng, Veronica 14 Gl–Goz 15 Gluck,
Louise 16 Gordimer, Nadine 17 Gordon, Mary 18 Gr–Gz 19 Gunn,
Thom 20 Gurganus, Allan 21 H–Haz 22 Hale, Nancy 23 Hall,
Donald 24 Hampl, Patricia 25 Handke, Peter 26 Hannah,
Barry 27 Hazzard, Shirley

FICTION CORRESPONDENCE, 1952–1980

373

887 1 2 Hecht, Anthony
3 Helprin, Mark 4 Hemenway, Robert 5 Ho–Hz 6 Hollander,
John 7 Howard, Richard 8 Hughes, Ted 9 I 10 Irving, John 11–12 J
13 Jhabvala, Ruth Prawer 14 Jong, Erica 15 Jordan, Neil 16 Just, Ward
17 Justice, Donald 18 K–Kez 19 Kanin, Garson

NEW YORKER RECORDS GUIDE

20 Keillor, Garrison 21 Ki–Kz 22 Kiely, Benedict 23 Kingston,
Maxine Hong 24 Kumin, Maxine
25–26 L-Lem 27 Le Guin, Ursula

FICTION CORRESPONDENCE, 1952–1980

374

888 1 2 Levine, Philip
3 Lewisohn, James 4 L'Heureux, John 5 Lorde, Audre 6 M–Maz
7 MacLeish, Archibald 8 Mamet, David 9 Mansfield,
Katherine 10 Mazor, Julian
11 McA–McZ 12 McCarthy, Mary 13 McElroy, Joseph 14 McEwan,

Ian 15 Me–Mi 16 Meehan, Thomas 17 Meredith, William 18 Merrill,
James 19 Merwin, W. S. 20 Mo-Mop 21 Molinaro,
Ursule 22 Mountzoures, H. L. 23–24 Mor–Mz 25 Munro, Alice
889 1 2 Nabokov, Vladimir
N
3 Nordan, Lewis 4 O 5 Oates, Joyce Carol 6 O'Brien, Edna 7 Ozick,
Cynthia 8 P–Phz 9 Paley, Grace

NEW YORKER RECORDS GUIDE

10 Percy, Walker 11 Pi–Pz 12 Pinsky, Robert 13 Plumly,
Stanley 14 Pound, Ezra
15 Pritchett, V. S. 16 R–Rz 17 Reid, Alistair 18 Rhys, Jean
19 Ri–Roz 20 Roethke, Theodore 21 Ru–Rz 22 Rudman,
Mark 23 S–Saz 24 Saroyan, William 25 Sarton, May 26 Sayles,
John 27 Sc–Sez 28 Settle, Mary Lee

FICTION CORRESPONDENCE, 1952–1980

375

890 1 2 Shelton, Richard
3 Simpson, Louis 4 Sissman, L. E. 5 Sm-Spz 6 Smiley, Jane
7 St-Stez 8 Stafford, William 9 Steegmuller, Frances 10 Sti–
Sz 11 Strand, Mark 12 Sullivan, Frank 13 Swan, Jon 14 Swenson,
May 15 T–Toz 16 Taylor, Peter 17 Theroux, Alexander 18 Theroux,
Paul 19 Tr–Tz 20 Tullius, F. P. 21 Tyler, Anne 22 U–V
Sh-Slz

NEW YORKER RECORDS GUIDE

23 Updike, John 24 Van Duyn, Mona 25 Vivante, Arturo 26 W–
Waz 27 Walcott, Derek 28 Walker, Ted 29 Warner, Sylvia Townsend
30 Warren, Robert Penn

FICTION CORRESPONDENCE, 1952–1980

376

891 1 2 White, Edmund
3 Wideman, John Edgar 4 Wilbur, Richard 5 Wo–Wz 6 Woiwode,
Larry
7 Wolff, Tobias 8 Wright, Charles 9 Wright,
James 10 X-Y-Z 11 Yevtushenko, Yevgeny

Phyllis Diller?

It's hard to say what is more daunting here—the vastness of
the archives, the enormous literary distinction they represent, or

the feudal-seeming cataloguing system. I leave. But not before yet another librarian stops by to visit and shows me how to go online and research the archives at my leisure—and possibly sedated, I'm thinking—and order boxes in advance. These listings are like a glass window behind which the overall magnificence and singularity of the institution of *The New Yorker* are on full display, and up against which my face is now mashed. It disables the ironic-distance function of my brain: OK—it's great, no matter all its eccentricities, mistakes, indulgences, superior attitudes masked by modesty. I don't even hate to admit it, and I feel very lucky to have been part of it.

Anyway, in view of this overwhelming display, I switch my research focus to my own papers. To call them "papers" is like calling a dog's breakfast crème brûlée. I go back up to the country, where my crème brûlée is moldering, but start using the Library's online search capability so I can order at least a few randomly representative boxes for later on, if I dare to go back. I look through "my" years—1969 through 1984. Guess whose name I look for first in the index. Now guess whose name is nowhere to be found. But it's probably in there somewhere. Because I worked with some of the writers named—Mavis Gallant, Harry Montzoures, V. S. Pritchett, Peter De Vries, Alice Adams, Frank Conroy, Ted Walker, Sylvia Townsend Warner—and because files like "Me–Mz" may well contain the odd note to or from me, or a galley or legal query or payment note I might have passed along.

But it all still seems like too much. So I go offline, and in between dog walks (and, as always these days, awaiting my next follow-up thoracic CT scan, which will show whether the radiation therapy last winter has worked or whether I'll be fucked sooner rather than later), I root around in the files and folders I took with me when I left the magazine and have continued to collect ever since. They are Lilliputian to the Library's Gulliverian, but still too plenteous, and also disorganized.

In the scrum of these documents, I find nostalgia, occasional straight-setting, re-inflammation, and amusement — or all four:

- A piece by the novelist and short-story writer Andre Dubus — whom I edited at *The New Yorker* — in the November 1977 issue of *Boston* magazine. It's about publishing short fiction in magazines and quarterlies in general and, climactically, in *The New Yorker*. About, at its most emotional moment, the magazine's often opulent advertising: "What angers me is seeing art juxtaposed with advertisements for things that have no use at all except to decorate the body, to turn people into Christmas trees, to turn their vision away from where art is trying to take them." Later in the piece, he says, of his current *New Yorker* editor, who is almost certainly me, "The man at *The New Yorker* loves commas more than Henry James did, but he never inserted one without asking my permission."

- A note from Helen Wolff — a well-known and highly respected editor, especially of books in translation, at the publishing house Harcourt Brace Jovanovich — that included a complaint from Max Frisch, the internationally acclaimed Swiss writer whose novella *Man in the Holocene* appeared in *The New Yorker*. It came out well enough to move Frisch to say, in a quiet note later on, that it looked better in the magazine than it did in the book. But before that, when the text was first set into *New Yorker* galleys, Frisch told us, through Mrs. Wolff, "I have only one worry. *The New Yorker* takes it on itself to insert or eliminate spacing in the text. I have to insist, as a non-negotiable condition, that my text be printed with exactly the same spacing as in the German edition. The reason why: because I tried to make the reader visualize, by the typographical arrangements, the thought leaps of the protagonist, and his memory lapses. Please tell all concerned that this is of the utmost importance to me."

- A note from Harold Brodkey from 1988. I think it is a condolence letter about my father's death. The timing is right, but it's hard to tell: "Dear Dan, I believe that the way we are conceived as organisms—the long journey from that to here—insures that life not seem very real, so that we are always on the edge of heroism or madness—men, I mean—and our parents and then our wives and children point out to us how to live, or, rather, they keep some chant or mechanism going more or less of life is real. And then one of them dies. So it wasn't so real, and isn't, but then again, it is. I wish I could defend my notion that ordinary writing lies about things fatal to us and for us when life happens, and the opposite. But I can't defend it. My arguments in favor of life are all on the page, in that other language. One day, soon, if you want, we can talk. At the moment, I'm busy being a public fool, someone whose opinions I wouldn't believe if I wasn't me. —HB"

- The first manuscript page of that 1976 *New Yorker* book review by the renowned psychoanalyst Robert Coles—bedecked with my original editing, in pencil.

- An "opinion" on a story titled "Patterns," by Tama Janowitz. Shawn's pencil scrawl at the bottom says, "Miss Cravens from Shawn: Sorry, but I liked this far less than the rest of you did, and I don't find it funny. The paragraph on p. 5 that Menaker found virtuoso comic writing I find intolerably broad."

- Eight or nine handwritten letters from Alice Munro, one of them about "The Albanian Virgin," which was the centerpiece of *The New Yorker*'s first Fiction Issue:

Dan—

   I've made a few extra changes + condensed the man-talk, also did a bit more, as you suggested, to "characterize" Lottar. Hope you can read all this mess. I'd really like to see it when all the changes are made. Call me if there's anything I've done that you wonder about.

                                            —A

Isn't this a dandy for the checkers?
Albania!
Montenegro!
Joe Hill!
Perkin Warbeck!

Munro, one of the two greatest English-language short-story writers of our time (the other is William Trevor), matched and sometimes out-bowed an editor's deferential posture with a deferential approach of her own:

"Do you think 'Around the Horn' might work as a title? It's not quite accurate, but neither is 'Dorrie.'"

"I've added a few sentences here and there, just opening things out a little where I thought necessary. Do you think that OK?"

"I've done [this revision] in the handwriting + proofs way. Does anybody else do that? Please excuse—"

And she was always a complete delight to work with:

Funny: "The apartment is so *clean*. I go around picking up bits of lint off the carpet. A good contrast to Clinton, where we live in an old house with a fair amount of debris + the occasional squirrel in the attic, rat in the cellar. I bought white dishes and red place mats + *now* it's kind of elderly yuppiedom. But mountains, Douglas firs, etc."

Flirty: At a BEA (BookExpo America) meeting in Chicago, she said to me, "My daughter thinks you're handsome."

Tables-turning, in the kind of comforting praise that usually flows from editor to writer: "P.S. You really are a great help and comfort to me."

There are hundreds of other letters and notes and galleys and high-school report cards and college papers and pay stubs and journal entries and my M.A. thesis (on *Catch-22*—a kind of valedictory nose-thumbing at graduate school) and opinion sheets and memos from *The New Yorker* and Random House and HarperCollins and then Random House again. To say nothing of thousands of computer-archived emails and family photographs and documents and letters from my childhood, including notes written by my mother to her mother when she was a freshman at Bryn Mawr. They lie around on the desk, are jammed into flash drives, cover the raised platform in the maid's room of my apartment where my son's mattress used to be, sit on the kitchen-renovation-leftover Corfam slab spanning two two-drawer filing cabinets in the back bedroom in the country, shut away in those filing cabinets, boxed and shoved into closets, packed chaotically into three drawers of an old chest, along with backgammon boards and antique letter-dice games and their small leather canisters and poker-chip caddies and music boxes and Scrabble tiles so ancient that someone had to resort to a black marker to restore their legibil-

ity, maybe in particular for my purblind spinster-schoolteacher
cousin Sophie Menaker, who, well into her eighties, would try
to secrete two or three of her superfluousity of vowels back into
the tile bag and steal what she hoped were X, Q, J, or Z replace-
ments, with my uncle Enge yelling, "I saw that, Sophie—put them
back!," yelling because Sophie was nearly deaf, and she would
reply, "What?," in response to which my uncle would mutter, "She
heard me," three discarded TV remotes, a four-by-eight-inch autograph book called "Golden Floral Album," decorated with
slightly raised images of three gold, orange, and brown pansies on
a dark-brown background, and once the property of Lulu George,
of Lunenberg, Massachusetts, containing the exquisite flower-
illustrations-punctuated Palmer-method inscriptions of what one
assumes were Ms. George's classmates and friends, and which include, for example, the following:

> Friend Lulu, Lulu,
> > *When you are bending o'er the tub*
> > *Think of me before you rub.*
> > *If the water is too hot,*
> > *Cool it and forget me not.*
> Carrie Linville
> September 29, 1886

And:

> Your Friend,
> Fred W. Osgood
> Lunenberg Mass.
> May 6, 1890.

The floral autograph book looks like something Alice Munro
would use as the starting point for one of her stories. She might

take one of the names or inscriptions and use it as a prop in or the centerpiece of a narrative that would, as always with her work, dramatize the emotional anarchy that dwells in the human heart and so often bests our reason. Coincidentally, before I run across this ancient keepsake book, I have written to Munro for permission to use the quotes from her letters. And, more coincidentally yet, I get an email from Lisa Dickler Awano, who is more or less Munro's Boswell. She sends me a link to a piece she has written for the *New Haven Review* called "Kindling the Creative Fire: Two Versions of Alice Munro's 'Wood.'" I edited "Wood" when it appeared in *The New Yorker,* in 1980. It's about a man named Roy, a craftsman who likes to go out into the forest in Ontario and chop down trees that loggers have left behind. He uses the wood for the work he does. Both versions concern, centrally, an accident that Roy has which almost costs him his life. But the second version, which Munro published in a recent collection, *Too Much Happiness,* presents subtle variations in details and psychology, and Awano does a masterly job of analyzing these revisions and showing how both versions involve themes and symbols that pervade all of this author's work. And at one critical point, Awano says, Munro has said that she aims to "get as close as [she] can" in her writing to "what [she] see[s] as reality—the shifting complex reality of human experience." Whenever the protagonist or reader lands on what seems a conclusive point of view in a Munro story, it is soon challenged by an equal and opposite perspective. Characters confound their own, each other's, and the reader's expectations, setting up psychological complications and narrative tensions that feel authentic.

This is exactly what all my recollections, and now this domestic archeology, have established about myself—my formation, my education, my profession, my writing, my character. I daresay, like many if not most of us, I've been honest, conscientious, lazy, dishonest, direct, faithful, unfaithful, stoic, self-pity-ing, open, limited, wise, ignorant, confident, vindictive, forgiving, cowardly, brave, generous, selfish, "and et cetera," as my son used to say.

Still, if we give our lives any thought, especially when we're drawing nearer the end of them, we try to marry the opposites into a coherent whole. A life story that comprehends and su-persedes its contradictions and says *Ecce Homo,* or maybe *Echhh Homo*—almost certainly both.

Finally, I give up on the idea of any sort of thorough archival research—at the Library or here in these drawers and closets and file cabinets and boxes. Facts and more facts lurk in them numer-ously, but in enterprises like this, facts have as much and (more important) as little bearing on the truth as memory does.

On the strength of a note that William Shawn wrote to me on his dying day and that his son Wallace Shawn found among his par-ents' effects three or four years ago and sent to me, I finally ask Wallace if he will have lunch with me and talk about his father. This is what the note said (Shawn must have been ill, and I must have written to him):

> Dear Mr. Menaker:
>
> Thank you for your kind and friendly letter. As you might guess, it was extremely pleasant to hear from you. I hope you can work out a happy arrangement with the new people. I hope, too, that you will play an important part in shaping the magazine's future.
>
> Warm regards,
William Shawn

Wallace told me in an email that he remains fascinated by his father. As do many of us who lived during Shawn's long—over-long—*New Yorker* reign. Someone needs to write a book about such commanding figures and their after-effects on those of us who fall under their spell, evil and/or otherwise—the long-term bosses who work their way into our limbic systems, causing post-mortem dreams, fantasies, grudges, and gratitude for the rest of our lives. Especially dreams. Someone I know, who at one point was Shawn's designated successor—one of five or six of Shawn's jukes in the direction of stepping down—has told me recently, in a moment of uncharacteristic emotional self-revelation and vulnerability, "I hate Shawn. I still dream about him."

Wallace and I meet at a good Greek restaurant on Seventh Avenue and 55th Street. We conversationally circle around his father for half an hour, talking about what we have been up to recently, his acting, my time at Random House, and then we get to the point. I tell Wallace what he already knows, that his father and I didn't get along, and that the note he sent to me at almost literally the last minute struck me as a wonderful gesture of conciliation, especially since I had learned so much about editing and writing under his father's influence. "His main example was to read like a child—very curiously and carefully," I say. "But with the full intellectual sophistication of a brilliant adult. He asked questions that sort of nagged at the back of your mind but never came forward until he asked them. Like the way kids will ask, 'But *why* did Hansel and Gretel's father marry such a horrible woman after his wife died?'"

"With you," Wallace said, "I think he just wanted to make something right, and that's why he wrote to you. I think he felt that he had made a mistake. That's something he almost never admitted. And he needed to set it right. But he didn't send it, because he died soon afterward."

"I'm glad you found it, and thank you for sending it to me,"
I say.

Then I say, "I've always had some trouble with authority, except for a few people—William Maxwell—"

"Oh! Mr. Maxwell!" Wallace says.

I tell Wallace about calling his father at home one evening and
his mother talking me into reading to her the risqué passage in
one of Pauline Kael's columns—Mrs. Shawn's saying that it was
OK to read the passage to her, now that I was married.

Wallace smiles. We go on for a while—the lunch lasts more
than two hours. It has knit—unpicked—some bones. Maybe for
both of us.

Seventy and a half

I am sitting at my desk in our house in the country on a gray October day amid the atmosphere and physical artifacts of what, I
realize more and more fully as I work on this book, is a rich and
strange family history. And in turn the work on this book has
grown more urgent after the diagnosis, last spring, of recurrent
lung cancer. I have to decide, soon, after five sessions of chemotherapy, about further treatment. Radiological treatment versus
more surgery.

The Workmen's Circle cup bestowed on my grandfather by
that organization for running his textile factory in New Jersey
on Socialist principles presides over the dining room, on top of
a piano. An antique squeeze-box that Uncle Enge played sits on a
dresser in one of the bedrooms. With a bigger accordion, he called
those square dances in the lodge of the camp he ran down on the
lake, where I spent my summers as a kid and then, as a teenager,
waited on tables. The tables—long, plain, sturdy—were on a
porch overlooking the lake, Lake Buel, named after Samuel Buel,

who in the nineteenth century saved a drowning man there. My handsome brother smiles at me from a black-and-white photograph—above a small bookcase near this computer I'm working on—taken for his graduation from Dartmouth, in 1959. In the bookcase, between an anthology of *New Yorker* short fiction about New York City, which I published at Random House, and a paperback edition of Don DeLillo's *Underworld* stand a first edition of John O'Hara's *A Rage to Live,* also published by Random House, in 1949, and a pamphlet called "Hard Hats and Hard Facts," by the head of the Communist Party in the Fifties and Sixties, Gus Hall. On a table near the front door is a stereopticon with a box of double-image stereographs—of the Grand Canyon, of the Amazon, of steam locomotives—that go along with it. Mexican *barro negro* ("black clay") pottery, from my uncle's winter trips to Mexico, fills the shelves of the sideboard in the dining room. (He and my father, who traveled in "Souse" America for business and some kind of low-grade Communist espionage, taught me a lot of Spanish.) A photograph of my grandfather Solomon, as a young man with burning, Revolutionary eyes, is propped on the wall on top of a picture of my six uncles as strapping young men standing in front of a hay wagon, looking like Young Soviet Farmers. Old books of home remedies for cancer—their provenance no doubt being Mr. Downs—gather dust in bookshelves next to urns straight out of Poe containing ashes of divers relatives who I imagine are silently judging what goes on here. A chest of drawers on the balcony above the kitchen holds 78 rpm albums, and hundreds of photographs, including one I have just found of my father and mother standing in front of an old station wagon, with me and my brother in front of them, and Timmy, my uncle's dog, in front of us. Sheet music from the Twenties and Thirties with Art Nouveau illustrations in a wooden box, along with old issues of *Sing Out!,* the folk-music journal from fifty, sixty years ago.

Just down the road, on the land once occupied by my uncle's boys' camp, lies a development called To-Ho-Ne Shores, after my uncle's camp. The developer named the road that loops through it Peter Menaker Road. ("You're *proud* of that?" a Southern country musician once asked me. "Hell, around here we're so inbred that it would be embarrassin'.") And just today I took Maxwell for a walk on that road, all but deserted now that the summer is over. We ran into a couple walking their dog, a black Lab puppy, and she and Maxwell tore up and down the road and across the lawns of now empty houses, and the couple wanted to know all about my family—the history of the place where they live.

And the New York of the Forties and Fifties feels, in retrospect, just as rich and romantic. The nation and its culture seemed robust and coherent. Only 140 million people. Joe DiMaggio in center field, Roosevelt on the radio, Communists and Red-baiters, new forms of jazz, *King Solomon's Mines* in movie theaters, frozen vegetables, pea shooters. That blond girl on top of me. One evening, at 290 West 4th, there was a knock at the door and I opened it and there stood a truly ugly man. My parents had sublet the top floor of the brownstone to a Welsh children's-book author named Ruthven Todd. The ugly man asked for Mr. Todd and went upstairs to visit. The ugly man, a "boily boy" by his own description, was Dylan Thomas.

Even *Fortune* magazine had its romance. I often visited my mother's office on school holidays and threw paper airplanes out the window of the Empire State Building. She worked with John Kenneth Galbraith and Walker Evans and Dwight Macdonald and James Agee. She also knew the Ashcan artist Reginald Marsh, who did covers for *Fortune*. As I've said, I believe she had an affair with him. There is a watercolor by Marsh in my apartment in New York of my mother modestly raising her skirt and wading in the ocean at Point Pleasant, New Jersey. Its inscription reads, "Mary

Grace, at the shore, 1929.—R. Marsh." There is that other Marsh in our living room—a painting of a garbage man with a broom and a white trash bin on wheels at a Greenwich Village corner—hanging like a high-culture reprimand above the flat-screen TV. We lived first at 50½ Barrow Street, in the Village. It was around the corner from Chumley's, a bar that had been a speakeasy and was hard to find—no sign. When it was a speakeasy, my handsome, charming, feckless Marxist father proposed there to my WASPY Bryn Mawr Classics-major mother.

I sit at the desk and remember: blackouts, which were practice for German air raids, and dim-outs, to save power and to keep ships in the harbor from becoming submarine-target silhouettes. My mother berating my father for bribing a butcher to get more meat than rationing allowed. FBI men—tall, rectangular, behatted—coming to talk to my father. High tension in the house. The sliding doors between the living room and dining room rumbling closed. That very tall FBI man named Tom McDade taking off his jacket and my staring at the huge gun in the shoulder holster he wore. His leaning over to me, from what seemed like a high, thin altitude, and asking me if I wanted to hold the gun. Tom found that my father's involvement with the Party was largely romantic and ineffectual, and I believe kept the House Un-American Activities Committee from calling him to testify. He became a friend of the family and built a house near my uncle's house, now my house, and his son and his family come up here to this day. When I was about fourteen, Tom showed me how to shoot that gun. It felt as heavy as an anchor.

I look at an old and out-of-tune upright piano. My father's side of the family had a musical gene. Uncle Enge learned how to play the piano from watching others do it. He could do it while being held upside down and backward to the keys. (He was short.) My father played the mandolin. I guess I inherited the gene, be-

cause at seven or eight I would sit in the living room listening to
Beethoven symphonies broken up by the dropping of one of the
stack of 78 rpm records on top of another, and I would get furious
if I was disturbed. The interrupted music was bad enough. I took
piano lessons and was good at them but insisted on stopping after a while. My mistake. I did learn to play the guitar a little from
Enge and then in college. Folk music abounded in the Village in
the Forties, especially at the Village Vanguard. Josh White, Leadbelly, Pete Seeger—who first didn't and then decades later did
remember Enge—alone and with the Weavers, appeared all the
time. I didn't understand it then, but Leadbelly taught me something about race and music that I didn't know and wouldn't really
hear again until I found early rhythm and blues on the radio and
then Bo Diddley.

When I was a kid, my mother, the *Fortune* editor, sometimes had
to go out to Chicago to talk to one of the company's executives,
whom I knew only by the name Fitz. I now feel certain that there
was something going on. When she died, I found a stack of letters
tied up in red yarn on the high shelf of her closet with a note on
the top saying, "Please destroy." They were lyrical love letters in
elegant handwriting—"When I think of you, my lovely Mary, my
heart thrills with excitement and I wish you were in my arms"—
and I bet they were from Fitz, though none were signed. I threw
them out—I was sure I threw them out, that is, until they sur-
faced again in one of the boxes when we moved from one apartment to another in New York. I don't know where they are now.
Everywhere I turn these days, especially when I am here in the
country, and the earth is thawing, and Maxwell, in many ways a
puppy still, full of beans, has his nose down to it, appreciating its
chilly aromas, and I wait for the results of some scary tests, I think

of my mother and her lover and how quickly we and what we do and say and whom we love all come and go.

My hair has grown thicker and curlier, the way it was before I started chemotherapy, and after I finished the subsequent stereotactic body radiation therapy, more than eight months ago now. It has been close to a year of treatments for the four malignant nodules in the lower lobe of my left lung. I'm not sure there is anything left to be said or even thought about cancer and its world, but, well, write what you know, and anyway, the experience of serious illness is always as varied in its complexities as its victims: the violent leg cramps at night after treatment with cisplatin, when you feel demons in the back of your thigh tying the muscles there into Ashley's stopper knots, the manic episodes caused by steroids administered to lessen the toxic effects of chemotherapy—I bought this computer when I was first on steroids (when my wife took them for hearing loss, she tried to buy an apartment)—the awkward and moving moments of support and renewed friendships, the discreditable angry suspicion of charity that accompanies gestures of fence-mending, the beautiful nurses with their expert IV techniques and their $10,000-a-dose, ten minutes' worth of pemetrexed, the endless repetitions of full name and date of birth, the nausea suppressed by superb new medicines (Emend—$310 for three pills—and ondansetron), the pure and purely random luck of being able to afford the best doctors and hospitals, the learning, finally, of patience, which is what must be the reason for our being called "patients," the weirdness of surgeons with their scrawled third-grade-level drawings of what they're going to cut out of you, the huge, futuristic radiology machines with rotating round cyclopean "eyes" that look like white sunflowers from another planet and whose radiation not only targets lesions in the lung and conforms to their shapes, thus sparing healthy tissue, but by means of instant feedback *moves* in order to adjust for breathing, the claustrophobia of some of those machines, especially the whole-body obese-cannon-like PET scanner, which takes almost an hour to ferry you through its noisy tube, halting for minutes and minutes and minutes at a time while one benzo or another just barely keeps panic away, the Pandora "stations" you request during radiation sessions (choose Hank Williams, I say), the recognition that ultimately, like the rest of us, the doctors sometimes don't know what they're doing, the botching that is almost bound to happen at one point or another—in your case, a second percutaneous needle biopsy (through your back and into your lung, to sample a lone nodule slightly removed from the others), which led to a pleural effusion, fluid outside the lung, which held up radiation therapy because with the fluid sloshing around outside, the nodules weren't stable enough to target, and which, when it was aspirated—by a handsome doctor from India who tucked his tie in between two of his shirt buttons, thus precipitating a huge crush on the part of your wife, who actually wanted to *watch* the needle go into your back— turned out to be six ounces of stuff that looked like cherry Kool-Aid, the question of when to tell your kids about what's going on, the insurance paperwork, the small vacations, like sabbaticals, between treatments, the alternating mortality depression and exhilaration, the latter, according to your therapist friend, proceeding from the unconscious conviction that you now have finally been punished enough for your sins, the increased recklessness of your discourse, the taking of taxis when you could easily take the subway or a bus, the miserliness you often feel about giving time to help others.

Some common perplexities: how to respond to the searching "No, really, how *are* you?"s after you've already answered "OK," the medical conversations in advance of which you write down and then during which ask every possible question, only to have seventeen more, proceeding from the answers you've just gotten, occur to you after you leave the doctor's office, one "How long?" after another from you, the interpretation, even by non-hypo-chondriacs, of lumps, bumps, sore throats, headaches, backaches, and rashes as possible metastases, the effort to keep up with new scholarly journal articles, of which you understand maybe fif-teen per cent, the belief in statistics when they're in your favor and their dismissal when they're not.

And then there's the intense cherishing of the spring when it comes—it is in full swing as I write this, with cherry blossoms in Riverside Park which look like white and pink lace from far away—the effort to forgive enemies, the savoring of sweets and other dietary easements, the dear children, your own and oth-ers' but especially your own, the gratitude for their virtues and the gratitude for their flaws, the simultaneous detachment from and appreciation of the quotidian, the intensified appreciation of great literature and good crappy movies, the strengthened fel-low-feeling with the soil as you turn it over for planting, accom-panied, paradoxically, by heightened wonder about abstractions: consciousness, will, randomness, time, the existence of anything rather than the far more logical nothing. Almost more than any-thing else, the sudden and almost absolute inconsequentiality of most daily decisions—whether to start the dishwasher now or later, accept or decline an invitation, watch *The Good Wife* or that other thing on AMC, cancel a dentist appointment, forswear steak for salmon, finish reading a book, let the dog off the leash, wear the same shirt again, allow a tepid friendship to dissipate, fill the car with gas when the tank is half empty, shop, cook, or order out, worry about the stock market, file for an extension, seek oth-ers' good opinion in small transactions, return a call, work out, sleep in, man up, lie down, give to, accept from, go before, follow after, think through, act on, let lie.

Which seems like a good idea at this point. Except maybe for a health update in an Epilogue. I don't have the years needed to do a thorough job of research and confirmation. The New York Public Library archives and my personal memorabilia frightened me with their subatomic detail. Anyway, a full autobiography, which such a substantiated work would be, differs greatly from a memoir. Memwah. Memoirs by their very etymology depend not on paper and physical artifacts but on memory. No wonder we don't trust them entirely, even when their authors do their best to be honest, as I have done here. Do we trust our own memories? We may when we're young, before they've piled into our brains and started bickering with each other, but we don't when we're older. Which I am. I remember sitting in the kitchen of The Farmhouse last spring—the kitchen where my uncle fried cottage-cheese blintzes on a huge, black Garland stove and railed against profit—and hearing someone on the radio reminding all of us to set our clocks ahead for Eastern Standard Time. He said, "The sun stays with us an hour longer today than it did yesterday." But of course it didn't—the sun pays no attention to us whatsoever.

Epilogue

Temporarily Firmer

Seventy-one

A three-bay open carriage shed stands about thirty feet south of the house—"The Country House," as Will refers to it. It always sounds like an official name. I *still* think of it as The Farmhouse or, just as often, Enge's House. The carriage shed, like the ancient corn crib near it and the huge red barn out in back, has seen better days. For some time, the four white posts that held it up in front were rotted at the base, like incisors going bad. The roof swooped down toward the middle, graceful but lowering. My wife and I finally decided that with some money to spend and with my medical circumstance and with our kids employed and with the imagined avuncular disapproval of the shed's condition reaching us from the Other Side, the Workers' Paradise—"I knew you couldn't keep this place up, boy"—we would have the building fixed.

I call the guy who has done some work for us in the past. He says it's not for him, but he knows the perfect person for it. Another guy, named Bruce, who loves to work on shoring up old buildings like this.

Bruce, a big, bearish man with a constant congenial smile and a shy affect, comes to check out the situation. After looking around the shed, inside and out, front and back, he says to me, gazing off into the distance, "I'm not going to lie to you, Daniel. I can fix this barn up so that it will outlive both of us for around ten thousand dollars, including materials."

Given lung cancer, the promise of the shored-up building outliving me is small comfort. But outliving *him!* That's different. A man in his late forties, I would guess. Now, that's worth 10K.

He does the work. It looks wonderful, even though the new blond boards around the shed's bottom stand out from the old, gray weathered ones higher up. That contrast will lessen over time. *Time Will Darken It* is the name of one of William Maxwell's novels. Bruce says to me, both of us standing in front of the shed, and again gazing away, "I'm not going to lie to you, Daniel, but clearing around the barn cost more than I expected. You can see here . . . and here . . . and over there the big boulders we ran into. It all comes out to about two thousand dollars more. I can keep my promise of ten thousand, but—"

"It's OK," I say. "A twenty per cent overrun is comparatively small potatoes when it comes to contracting, isn't it? And I can see the extent of the extra work with my own eyes."

"I like you, Daniel," Bruce says.

After Hurricane Sandy, I notice that the white sliding doors at the back of the big red barn have fallen down—the barn is open to the elements and the fauna. I call Bruce. He comes over one weekend in November to take a look. "I'm very busy, Daniel," he says. "Working right next door at the Abelson house and then down the road at the Hawkins place. But it wouldn't be a big job to hang some new doors here on a new beam. We could also strengthen some of the posts. I like you, Daniel, and I could try to squeeze this in on Tuesday and Wednesday."

"I like you too, Bruce," I say, "and I would really appreciate that. How much do you think it will cost? And don't lie to me."

He laughs. "I won't, Daniel," he says. "I'd say eighteen hundred."

"Done," I say.

I have another follow-up CT scan in June of 2013. It's negative. I feel as though these wonderful physicians are Bruce's medical counterparts. Shoring me up against ill winds, extending my life considerably beyond where it would have ended without them, giving me temporarily firmer legs to stand on. But there is an important difference. Unlike the outbuildings at The Country House, and despite the medical problems I've had and have, and despite creaking around and forgetting names and all the indignities and infirmities of age, I have never seen better days. My children grown, employed, great fun to be with. My wife successfully launched on a new career of writing very good books after a lifetime's work as a great editor. Good friends, material comfort, fine coffee, *The Walking Dead, Breaking Bad, Searching for Sugar Man.* A whole fleet of young writers I worked with now approaching middle age and doing well.

The splendid improbability of the colorful outfit of the flicker on the bird feeder at The Country House. The music of J. E. Mainer available with the click of "Enter" on my computer.

This book finished. But, most radically, that amazing flicker, with his fiery red head feathers, his chevron plumage, and that stiletto beak.

I have never seen better days. No mistake.

Acknowledgments

Settle in.

Thank you to George Hodgman, the editor at Houghton Mifflin Harcourt, who acquired this book. He left a message on my answering machine that started, "Daniel Menaker, I am you," and he left the company shortly after that. But even though he was me, I stayed. A deal, it turns out, is a deal.

Thanks, then, subsequently, to Bruce Nichols, HMH's Publisher, for hanging on. And to Jenna Johnson, an excellent and sensitive reader who, even though she is not me, took over as editor. If I were in publishing still, I would try to poach her. And to Larry Cooper, a wonderful manuscript editor, who kept me from referring to a temperance pamphlet as an abolitionist pamphlet and saved my bacon in countless other ways, although he dared to compare Dom DiMaggio to Joe. And to Carla Gray, HMH's head of marketing, who invests in racehorses and makes all of her writers feel like Seabiscuit. And to everyone else at HMH for their revision forbearance, and their support, and the free beer and sort of ad hoc, darkling dinner at the Associated Writers Program conference in Boston earlier this year. (Eleven thousand writers in one place. Aieee.) And to Eric Hanson, who did the wonderful cover, spine, and endpapers for the book. He began to have second thoughts, as you can see from the drawing, but it was too late.

Thanks next to Judy Sternlight and Samuel Douglas, both of

whom made crucial suggestions about the structure, texture, and tone of the writing here, and however lame that foot may be, saw to it that I put my best foot forward. Larry, shouldn't it be "better foot forward," for bipeds?

James Gleick gets a separate paragraph, for suggesting, among many other deft, strict suggestions, that I take out the first eleven paragraphs of the Introduction as it stood when he read it. And for his quote there on the back. It's annoying (as he would say) that he can be such a good writer, friend, editor, and cook—and the smartest person I know—all at the same time.

Something tells me that Esther Newberg, my agent, also better get her own paragraph. So here it is. Thank you, Esther, for being such a great advocate and such a great friend (even though you yelled at me, quietly, about posting the rejections of this book on the *Huffington Post*). Just think of it—going on fifty years now. Well, maybe don't think of it. As you told me recently, comfortingly and disturbingly, "We can't die young anymore."

Thanks to Robert Gottlieb and Wallace Shawn for their invaluable *New Yorker* perspectives, and to Gillian MacKenzie for her advice about the book. And to Charles McGrath, for his friendship and unfailing good sense—generally, among many of the rest of us, in such short supply.

Thank you to Drs. Minna Fyer, Zachary Bloomgarden, Barbara Schultz, Siddhartha Mukherjee, Balazs Halmos, Gregory Riely, Andreas Rimner, Kent Sepkowitz, and Valerie Rausch—and everyone else at Memorial Sloan-Kettering Cancer Center—for your expertise and superb care.

My family—my wife, Katherine Bouton, and my kids, Will and Elizabeth: Thank you for every inestimable thing you've given me, except when you were three or four, Will, and gave me scarlet fever. Thanks even for that, come to think of it, as it kept me from smoking for seventy-two hours and I was then able to quit.